TO MATCH A DREAM

TO MATCH A DREAM

A PRACTICAL GUIDE TO CANADA'S CONSTITUTION

Deborah Coyne and Michael Valpy

M&S

Canadian Cataloguing in Publication Data

Coyne, Deborah M. R. (Deborah Margaret Ryland)
    To match a dream : a practical guide to Canada's constitution

Includes bibliographical references and index.
ISBN 0-7710-2277-8

1. Constitutional history – Canada.   2. Federal government – Canada.   3. Canada – Politics and government.   4. Constitutional law – Canada.   5. Federal-provincial relations – Canada.
I. Valpy, Michael, 1942- .   II. Title.

JL65.C69 1998   342.71´029   C98-931729-3

We acknowledge the financial support of the Government of Canada through the Book Publishing Industry Development Program for our publishing activities. We further acknowledge the support of the Canada Council for the Arts and the Ontario Arts Council for our publishing program.

Cartography: VISUTRONX Service Inc.
Typeset in Minion by M&S, Toronto
Printed and bound in Canada

McClelland & Stewart Inc.
The Canadian Publishers
481 University Avenue
Toronto, Ontario
M5G 2E9

1 2 3 4 5 6   03 02 01 00 99 98

CONTENTS

PREFACE

It's tough to build a country to match a dream.

— Pierre Trudeau

OUR PURPOSE IN WRITING this book is simple: We want
our fellow citizens to understand the constitutional debate
that has obsessed Canada's elites for more than two hundred
years, a debate lamentably expropriated by generations of
terminally solemn people given to speaking an obscure and
priestly language. Susan Delacourt, for many years *The Globe
and Mail*'s constitutional affairs reporter, once mused in a
fey and restless moment that the constitutional doctrine
of "concurrent jurisdiction with provincial paramountcy"
would be the phrase least likely to appear on a placard
should Canadians ever take to the streets in political rebellion. Which is to say that the language and the agendas of
the participants in Canada's constitution wars too often
obscure a fascinating history of the shaping of the supreme
rules that govern our country and hide the reality of what
has taken place.

We have written this book with love for Canada and its
special personality, if not particularly for those politicians,
bureaucrats, academics, and journalists who have felt obliged

to twist history and diminish the nation's existence for the ends of power and the objectives of the powerful.

We have written this book to demystify the issue, to explain what lies behind the words, where things come from, why some cherished slogans crumple beneath historical scrutiny. It is intended to be a primer and a guide. What is the origin of "distinct society" in Quebec? Was Confederation in 1867 a "pact" between "two founding peoples"? Do Canadians inhabit the most decentralized country on Earth – and, if they do, how did it happen and what does it mean? Was Quebec "left out" by the Constitution agreement of 1982? Why are we officially bilingual? What was wrong with the Meech Lake and Charlottetown constitutional accords? Are minority rights in Canada weakened by the Newfoundland constitutional amendment altering the role of churches in its public schools? Was the Constitution asymmetrical from its beginning? And, yes, what is concurrent jurisdiction with provincial paramountcy?

We have written this book to demonstrate that nothing about Canada's Constitution just *happened*. Nothing was suddenly invented by this or that government or by this or that bureaucratic or academic cabal. Nothing ever sprang naked, previously unknown and unformed, from a political party's manifesto in a given election year. The constitutional issues Canadians debate today – whether they be about language, minority rights, or federal and provincial powers – are, for the most part, rooted centuries deep. And to make sure that point is understood, our book (readers will note) rather clearly changes voice between the early chapters dealing with history and the later chapters dealing with issues. The opening narrative is a tale of origins, a collection of constitutional "Just So" stories about how things came to be, a light and amiable stroll around the fountainhead of beginnings. Access-easy constitutional history, in a phrase. Then, with history on board, the second part of the book is, well, not dry, but more of a no-nonsense, purposeful march through the Constitution's current framework and issues. Thus, if readers reach the last page feeling feistily able to insert "concurrent jurisdiction with provincial paramountcy" into a dinner-party conversation *with* a trenchant analysis of its deficits, we will be pleased.

Finally, we give thanks: to Michael Bliss, Ramsay Cook, and Robert Howse, who vetted our text for egregious errors (any that remain are most certainly our fault, not theirs), and to McClelland & Stewart publisher Douglas Gibson and senior editor Jonathan Webb who adroitly, patiently, and sensitively helped this project over obstacles.

CHAPTER 1

CONQUEST, SHOTGUN MARRIAGE

Canadians do not even share myths – those imagined truths that find acceptance because they illuminate the soul and galvanize the national will. In other words, Canadians refuse to share a common history. And so history, the collective remembrance of moments past, is not an emotional act in this country. It is largely a political one. I have decided to attempt to reverse that use of history.

The summer of 1759, culminating in the battle of the Plains of Abraham, which brought about the capitulation of the town of Quebec and its adjacent territory, is perfect for my purposes. It is the most important moment in our history. It is neither an English nor a French moment. It is a Canadian one, and we are all a part of it.

— Laurier LaPierre, 1759: The Battle for Canada

FIRST, THERE IS THE PAST. The year 1759 is used as the starting point of Canada's Constitution story. It is in some ways an arbitrary choice. Canadian constitutional history starts at many different points in many different years – for instance, with the centuries-old confederacy of the Iroquois League; with John Cabot's territorial claims on June 24, 1497, on behalf of England's Tudor king Henry VII; with the

Covenant Chain and Seven Fires accords between aboriginal peoples and French and English settlers; with the advent of French royal rule of the province of New France; with the great constitutional instruments of British history – Magna Carta and so forth – grafted onto Canada's Constitution by the common-law doctrine of "reception."

However, the wellspring of Canada's peculiar constitutional turbulence, still bubbling trouble today, is found on the morning of September 13, 1759. Just after 8 a.m., 4,500 French regular troops and civilian militiamen came out of the fortified city of Quebec to meet an equal number of British regular soldiers on a grassy field called the Plains of Abraham. The battle lasted scarcely fifteen minutes. It was the climax, more or less, to a lengthy British–French conflict throughout eastern and central North America, part of the global hostilities of the Seven Years War. It was, until the 1960s, rudely if unintentionally celebrated in English-speaking Canada in a solemn song that was almost an anthem, "The Maple Leaf Forever." Contemporary Quebec nationalists have labelled the battle "The Humiliation" and, only slightly less provocatively (but on both sides of the language divide), it is called "The Conquest."

History is not a product of what might have been, but of what has been. The Conquest presented Canada with its eternal dialectic. It determined that French-speaking Canadiens became, firstly, subjects of the British Empire and, subsequently, partners in a two-language state. This chapter explains why, constitutionally, there is a "French fact" to Canada. It follows the thread of constitutional development that begins with military rule in Quebec by a conquering alien army and leads on to the failed efforts to assimilate the Canadiens into an Imperial English world;

to recognition of French customs, institutions, and language; to the establishment of civil colonial rule; to the American Revolution and the resulting migration of English-speakers into what previously had been almost exclusively French-speaking territory; to the division of Quebec into two provinces – Upper and Lower Canada – largely determined by language; to rebellion in the two Canadas and the establishment of representative and responsible colonial government; and, finally, to the stage on which Confederation was framed and the nineteenth-century nation of Canada created. If readers find the story excessively focussed on the political and cultural tensions enveloping Quebec, they are reminded that it is those tensions which have shaped Canada's Constitution, shaped its basic law, and have given the Constitution its tone.

To quote Quebec political commentator Lysiane Gagnon: "Canada's history is not a love story. At worst, it is the story of an uncomfortable and rancorous relationship. At best, it is a story akin to that of two mature persons, each with a long, rich past, who decide to share a house because they have common interests and common values – and some common recent history."* Gagnon's definition, of course, is too limiting; there have always been more than two mature persons sharing the house. But whatever the relationship, at worst or at best, it is a fact of human nature that the participants hold selective memories of their past. Canada's constitutional story is fogged by many selective memories.

---

* *The Globe and Mail*, July 9, 1994

CANADA AT THE CONQUEST, 1759

The French colony of Canada along the St. Lawrence River at the time of the Seven Years War was ruled directly from the royal court at Versailles and kept highly dependent on the motherland, was unused to making decisions for itself, possessed a system of government that functioned successfully only as long as instructions and support were received from the other side of the Atlantic, and was defended largely by farmer-militiamen, whose avocation was not to make war, but to grow food.

The colony could not, in wartime, feed its 3,000 regular troops plus its aboriginal allies and civilian militia. The need for manpower to raise crops ruled out lengthy military ventures. The 60,000 Canadiens faced more than 1 million settlers in the British–American colonies to the south, a population disadvantage of nearly twenty to one. The American colonies were, to a great degree, self-governing. The quantity of foodstuffs and military *matériel* available to them was enormous. Pennsylvania alone could export enough food to the rest of the colonies to provide for an army of 100,000, and its iron industry competed with England's.

The civil government of François Bigot, last intendant (civil administrator) of New France, was undermined by massive corruption and administrative fraud. The divided responsibilities and personal conflicts between Pierre de Rigaud, Marquis de Vaudreuil, New France's last governor general, and his subordinate, Louis-Joseph de Montcalm, commander of French troops in North America, undermined the colony's military strength. In 1757, the prime-ministership of Britain passed to William Pitt the Elder, a man obsessed with driving the French from North America.

To James Wolfe, a ruthless thirty-two-year-old general,

fell the command of the British force sent to take Quebec. While he waited three months on the river below the city's high promontory, dithering over how to engage its garrison, he terrorized the surrounding, undefended agricultural community, burning 1,400 houses to the ground. This was the "dauntless hero" of English-Canadian song. Because the French had left undefended the south shore of the St. Lawrence opposite Quebec, Wolfe established batteries there which bombarded and largely destroyed the city. By luck, he discovered a path up the cliffs on the north shore, lightly guarded because Vaudreuil – thinking the ascent impossible for an army – had ordered one of Montcalm's regiments away from it for service elsewhere. At the top of the cliff, the British assembled outside the city's western wall, which had no gun emplacements. Without waiting for reinforcements from 3,000 regular troops stationed fifteen kilometres away, Montcalm ordered his surprised and disorganized soldiers to stream out of the city and attack. The highly trained British force waited until the French were forty metres away, then cut them down with two musket volleys followed by a bayonet attack. The French retreated in disarray. Wolfe and Montcalm both died of injuries received in the battle.

THE END OF FRENCH RULE, 1760
Although beaten at Quebec, the French retained control of the rest of the St. Lawrence valley. In April 1760, François-Gaston de Lévis, who had succeeded Montcalm as French commander-in-chief, defeated the British at Ste-Foy, immediately west of Quebec. It was a battle far bloodier than the one on the Plains of Abraham. Lévis besieged Quebec until

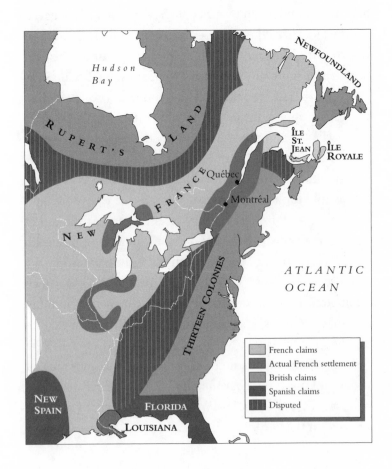

New France, 1713

British relief ships came up the river in May. He wanted to make a last stand against the British at unfortified Montreal – in the face of a British–American force vastly superior in numbers to his own – but was overruled by Governor General Vaudreuil, who gave up the city to spare the residents further suffering. The terms of surrender which Vaudreuil negotiated with the British military commander, General Jeffery Amherst, gave shape to a nation.

First, and most important, the Canadiens would not share the fate of deportation dealt out to the Acadians of Nova Scotia and the garrison and civilian community at Fort Louisbourg on Ile Royale (Cape Breton Island). There would be no immediate change in property rights (including the feudal seigneurial system established in 1627, under which the approximately two hundred seigneuries granted by the French regime provided the basis for the organization of the rural life of the "habitants," or tenants), the Roman Catholic religion (severely circumscribed in Britain), and the civil-law system (the Coutume de Paris, introduced in 1663 when the colony came under direct royal rule from France). Those residents who desired to return to France were allowed to do so, and most of the wealthy business people, government officials, and other elites did, leaving the habitants, their clergy, and the seigneurs to deal with the conquerors on their own. Thus, on September 8, 1760 – 226 years after Jacques Cartier first poked the bows of his two tiny ships into the indentations of the Labrador coast – Canada passed forever from France's rule.

BRITISH MILITARY RULE, 1760–1763

The defeat of the French in North America was probably inevitable. Aside from administrative disadvantages and military tactical errors, fortune favoured the larger army. Historians and political scientists continue to debate its significance. Popular histories of English-speaking Canada tend not to adequately appreciate that, by the date of the surrender of Montreal, nearly a quarter of the population of Canadiens had been under arms for five years. As much as one-tenth of the civilian population – six thousand people – were wartime casualties. Every community had suffered, in particular the area around Quebec City. In the most heavily populated parts of the colony, militiamen had gone home from war to find their crops destroyed, their livestock seized, and their houses burned. There had been widespread hunger and disease. The colony was economically devastated.

Quebec's first major historian, the nineteenth-century nationalist François-Xavier Garneau – who put voice to the ideals that guided French-Canadian nationalists until the mid-twentieth century – portrayed the Conquest as the beginning of his people's "sufferings and humiliations." Other historians, both francophone and anglophone, have written that the Conquest removed the Canadiens from absolute subjection under France's Bourbon kings, ushered them into a political life of constitutional government, and spared them the social and institutional chaos of the French Revolution. Moreover, the case can be made that the Conquest's biggest losers were not the Canadiens at all, but the aboriginal peoples. The end of the Anglo-French conflict in North America debased their value to both sides as warrior-allies and made them increasingly irrelevant to white society.

THE ROYAL PROCLAMATION, 1763

The Treaty of Paris of 1763 formally ended the Seven Years War. By its terms, all French territory in northeastern North America (except the tiny island group of Saint-Pierre and Miquelon in the Gulf of St. Lawrence) was ceded to Britain. This included Canada (Quebec), Ile Royale (Cape Breton Island), Ile Saint-Jean (Prince Edward Island), and the territory of modern New Brunswick. (Britain had earlier acquired from the French – in 1713 – the Nova Scotia peninsula.) The British were not sure they wanted Canada. Prime Minister Pitt asked: "Some are for keeping Canada, some Guadaloupe. Who will tell me what I shall be hanged for not keeping?" In the end, for reasons of military security, Britain decided on Canada.

The Royal Proclamation of 1763, signed by George III, established the administrative framework for the newly acquired territory. It was an exercise of what is known as the sovereign's prerogative power (under English common law at the time, the sovereign could legislate alone – without Parliament – for conquered colonies) and is one of the most incendiary and possibly one of the least understood documents of Canadian constitutional history. Ostensibly, its objective was to impose uniform, orderly administrative management on all of Britain's North American colonies. In reality, its purpose was to encourage English-speaking settlement in Quebec by discouraging the growth and maintenance of a distinct French society. This, to the British, was the most logical means of nurturing order and loyalty in Canada in the event of renewed Anglo-French hostilities.

Out of New France, the Royal Proclamation created the Crown colony (or province) of Quebec, which was defined as the Gaspé peninsula and a quadrilateral-shaped territory enclosing the valley of the St. Lawrence River. (The area had been referred to as "Canada," and the inhabitants remained known as "Canadien.") The Proclamation replaced military rule with civilian rule by a governor and appointed executive council. It promised an elected assembly ("so soon as the state and circumstances . . . will admit thereof") after the style of elected assemblies already functioning in Nova Scotia and the thirteen American colonies. It introduced English law, to be supplemented by local legislative acts (acts "as near as may be agreeable to the Laws of England and under such Regulations and restrictions as are used in other Colonies"). It empowered all colonial governors to introduce "Courts of Judicature and Public Justice within our said Colonies for hearing and determining all Causes, as well Criminal as Civil, according to Law and Equity, and as near as may be agreeable to the Laws of England." There was to be freedom of religion, but only "so far as the laws of Great Britain permit" – meaning Roman Catholics were barred from participating in government – and the first civilian governor of Quebec, James Murray, was instructed to establish and promote Anglicanism. In sum, the Royal Proclamation and ancillary British government policy intentions built a wall between Roman Catholic Canadiens and the state, and denied them their laws, courts, and customary regulation of commerce.

The Royal Proclamation also designated the Labrador coastline as part of Newfoundland and set a western boundary for both Quebec and the Thirteen Colonies, beyond which European settlement was prohibited and the lands reserved for the "several nations or tribes of Indians" under the King's "protection" – the "Indian Territory" mythologized in so many American films. (The boundary in Quebec was a north–south line between Lake Nipissing and the point where the 45th parallel crosses the St. Lawrence.) Furthermore, the proclamation decreed that aboriginal land rights could be sold only to the Crown, thus placing aboriginal territory beyond the reach of European land-grabbers. Because of these two provisions (boundary and land-sale restrictions) protecting aboriginal territory, the Royal Proclamation has been called the First Nations' Magna Carta and the First Peoples' Bill of Rights. Current debates, legal arguments, and court decisions concerning aboriginal self-government, treaty rights, land-claim settlements, and fishing and hunting rights continue to refer to and rely upon the Proclamation.

OUTCOME OF THE ROYAL
PROCLAMATION, 1763–1774
The Proclamation violated the principle of English common law that a colony acquired by conquest or by cession should continue to enjoy its pre-existing private law (except in matters involving the relationship between the inhabitants and the sovereign), while its public law – the establishment of governmental institutions – should correspond to British practice. The edict that British justice and laws, including property laws, were to replace the traditional French "customs and usages" permitted under British military rule created chaos in the Canadiens' affairs. Their exclusion from public life added to the colony's administrative difficulties. Protestant anglophone immigration did not occur, apart from the arrival of two hundred shifty merchants and camp-followers ("Licentious Fanaticks," in Governor Murray's words) who moved into Quebec behind the British

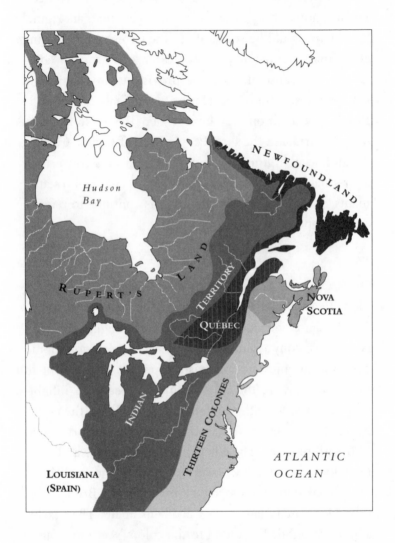

Eastern North America at the time
of the Royal Proclamation

army and immediately began demanding all the instruments of British governance promised by the Proclamation, including an elected assembly which they would have controlled. The Roman Catholic Church, the one institution spared anglicization, quickly acquired an importance in the colony which hitherto it had not possessed. And the Proclamation's proscription of westward expansion was to become one of the causes of the American Revolution, an event with a profound impact on Quebec.

Governor Murray resisted the Proclamation's provisions. He appointed only a small executive council. He slowly introduced English civil law into the colony, while permitting the continued use of French law and customs in the courts. He took it upon himself to waive prohibitions against Roman Catholics serving on criminal-trial juries or practising as lawyers. He refused to create an elected assembly. Rather than promoting Anglicanism, he sought to make the Roman Catholic Church an ally, arranging for a new bishop to be chosen (the previous one had died) and sent to France for consecration. He wrote to the British Lords of Trade (who oversaw colonial affairs) on October 29, 1764:

> Little, very little, will content the New Subjects [the Canadiens] but nothing will satisfy the Licentious Fanaticks Trading here, but the expulsion of the Canadians who are perhaps the bravest and the best race upon the Globe, a Race, who cou'd they be indulged with a few privileges which the Laws of England deny to Roman Catholicks at home, wou'd soon get the better of every National Antipathy to their Conquerors and become the most faithful and most useful set of men in this American Empire.

I flatter myself there will be some Remedy found out even in the Laws for the Relief of this people, if so, I am positive the populer clamours in England will not prevent the Humane Heart of the King from following its own Dictates . . . certain I am, unless the Canadians are admitted on Jurys, and are allowed Judges and Lawyers who understand their Language his Majesty will lose the greatest part of this Valuable people. . . .

Murray preferred the company of the refined seigneurs and their families – with whom he could converse in excellent French – to the English tradesmen, "the most cruel, ignorant, rapacious fanaticks whoever existed." The merchants, in turn, considered Murray a despot and petitioned the King for his removal. In June 1766, he sailed to England, and though he cleared his name and officially remained governor until 1768, he never returned to Quebec. He was succeeded by Guy Carleton, who within a very short time endorsed Murray's policies of strengthening the Roman Catholic Church, of permitting commercial cases in the courts to be adjudicated according to the Coutume de Paris, and of resisting the creation of an elected assembly. Carleton declared that Quebec was French and would remain so: "Barring a catastrophe . . . this country must, to the end of time, be peopled by the Canadian race." As Britain's colonies to the south grew more rancorous and rebellious, he saw Quebec as an island of social and political stability in an increasingly stormy sea. He argued that there was little point in trying to assimilate the Canadiens into a fractious Empire. He persuaded the British government – in the face of threats from the British merchants in Quebec to economically ruin the colony should Carleton's recommendations be acted upon – that what was needed in Quebec were not British institutions, but recognition of existing French institutions, which would bind the Canadiens more closely to the Empire.

QUEBEC ACT, 1774

Influenced both by Carleton and by the growing unrest in the American colonies, the British government acknowledged that the Royal Proclamation was "inapplicable to the state and circumstances of the colony [Quebec]." Parliament therefore enacted the Quebec Act, 1774, which Carleton largely framed and which revoked the Proclamation with the exception of its provisions for aboriginal peoples. Thus, ninety-three years before Confederation and the formation of the Canadian federalist state, the Quebec Act created the legal foundation of French Canada's survival in North America.

It was not all that it appeared. It was motivated more by Britain's desire to maintain a secure, stable anchor on the northern flank of the restless American colonies than by enlightened magnanimity toward the Canadiens. It was accompanied by secret instructions to Carleton to continue the work of assimilating the Canadiens into British life and of undermining their customs and institutions. But it did restore pre-Conquest French civil law to Quebec and, in so doing, made Quebec well-defined within the British Empire, a status designed "for the more perfect Security and Ease of the Minds of the Inhabitants of the said Province."

The legislation was called "an Act for making more effectual Provision for the Government of the Province of Quebec in North America." It removed restrictions on

Roman Catholics holding public office by excusing them from swearing an oath acknowledging the sovereign as head of the church (the sovereign, at the time, was head of the Anglican Church in Canada and elsewhere, but not, of course, of the Roman Catholic Church). It permitted the clergy of both the Roman Catholic and Protestant (i.e., Anglican) churches to collect "accustomed Dues and Rights." It stated that "all His Majesty's Canadian subjects within the Province of Quebec . . . may also hold and enjoy their Property and Possessions, together with all Customs and Usages relative thereto, and all other their Civil Rights . . . as if the said Proclamation [the Royal Proclamation of 1763] . . . had not been made" – meaning the seigneurial system of land tenure, including payment of seigneurial dues, was enshrined in law, and the French Coutume de Paris would be the civil law in Quebec side by side with English criminal law. It authorized the governor to appoint a legislative council of between seventeen and twenty-three members "to make Ordinances for the Peace, Welfare and good Government of the said Province" with the governor's consent. It declared that it was "at present inexpedient to call an Assembly." (The British government wanted neither an elected body controlled by Canadiens nor one controlled by the British merchant community, now numbering about five hundred persons, and the Canadiens themselves, for the most part, were cool to the idea.)

It enlarged the province's boundaries on the east to include Labrador, Ile d'Anticosti, and the Iles de la Madeleine, and extended Quebec's western frontier into the "Indian Territory" between the Mississippi and Ohio rivers. This was a piece of geopolitical map-drawing the British much liked because it boosted Quebec's struggling economy by granting its fur traders (the principal source of the colony's wealth) privileged access to the new territory, acknowledged that the Quebec traders had generally good relations with the aboriginal peoples, and gave the British an added presence in the heart of the continent.

OUTCOME OF THE QUEBEC ACT, 1774–1775

The formal statutory protection of French civil law and the denial of an elected assembly enraged the British merchants. Canadien farmers were disappointed with the legal recognition given tithes and seigneurial dues (although they were likely pleased by the restoration of a system that enabled them to obtain land without paying for it). The British government was frankly duplicitous. While publicly it spoke of granting the Canadiens "more perfect security" with the Quebec Act, it secretly instructed Carleton to seek ways of introducing English civil law. It also gave him detailed instructions to subordinate the Roman Catholic Church to state control by means of regulation and repression of religious orders (with state confiscation of their assets), permission for priests to marry, official review of the bishop, prohibition against appeals to any "foreign ecclesiastical jurisdiction" (meaning the Pope), and provision for Protestant clergy at some future date to collect tithes from non-Protestants. The Roman Catholic bishop of Quebec learned of the secret instructions and confronted Carleton, who assured him that he disapproved of them and intended to ignore them. As for the Americans, they accurately interpreted the Quebec Act as a measure that continued to seal off the West and they resented the religious tolerance it extended to Roman Catholics. The statute was designated

as one of the "Intolerable Acts" that ignited the American
Revolution the following year.

THE AMERICAN REVOLUTION
AND THE LOYALISTS, 1775–1791

The alliance of France with the American colonists in 1778,
three years into the revolutionary war, influenced its outcome. A secret clause in the French–American arrangements
stipulated that France should not invade Quebec or Acadia;
there was no desire in either the incipient United States or
the former mother country for a revived New France. As
for the world inside the St. Lawrence colony, the Canadiens'
interest, like the aboriginal peoples' interest, in a war where
both sides were English was slight. Neither group could
foresee that a revolutionary victory would create modern
Canada as well as an American republic.

In the newly independent United States the victors'
bitterness toward those of their fellow former colonists
who had desired to remain loyal to the British Crown led
to severe persecution. Men and women were imprisoned,
whipped, tarred and feathered, dragged through horse
ponds. Many were hanged. The property of hundreds was
confiscated for no crime other than their support of a lost
cause. The result was a migration of more than forty thousand Loyalists to Canada. Most were farmers, neither well-
to-do nor high in social rank (although they quickly claimed
that status). Many were recent immigrants to America.
Some brought slaves with them. Some were free blacks and
escaped slaves. At least two thousand Mohawk allies of the
British were dispossessed and became, reluctantly, part of
the Loyalist trek north. The revolutionary war, in fact,

fractured the Iroquois Confederacy, of which the Mohawks were the most eastern members. The Americans refused to recognize the boundaries of the Indian Territory. The Treaty of Paris of 1783, which formally ended the war with Britain, made no mention of aboriginal peoples. The British ceded to the Americans sovereignty over the Indian Territory even though the Iroquois, whose land it was, had never acknowledged direct British sovereignty over it or the Crown's right to dispose of it.

About thirty thousand Loyalists went to the Maritimes, subsequently creating the separate colony of New Brunswick (and, later, of Prince Edward Island). They fit well into the Maritimes, where the existing population was either satisfied with British institutions already in place – including an elected assembly in Nova Scotia controlled by the Halifax merchants – or too distant from political power to do anything about them.

About ten thousand Loyalists travelled to Quebec and remained there, despite the efforts of the governor (Frederick Haldimand, who replaced Carleton in 1777 and served until 1786) to persuade them to move on to the Maritimes. Two thousand settled in the Gaspé, the seigneury of Sorel on the Richelieu River, and in what was to become the Eastern Townships. The remaining eight thousand accepted Haldimand's encouragement to settle in the far west of the province, along the north shore of Lake Ontario, well removed from the centres of French population. Haldimand rightly feared conflicts between English and French over land governed by seigneurial tenure. Thus, north of Lake Ontario (and west of the seigneurial lands), the British government set aside three million acres for Loyalist settlement. Each family was offered two hundred freehold acres plus provisions, seeds, tools, and transportation costs, and a promise that as much land would be given to each son on coming of age and each daughter upon her marriage. (Many "late Loyalists" who arrived to take up the offer were more land-grabbing opportunists than loyal.)

"Barring a catastrophe," Carleton had prophesied, "this country must, to the end of time, be peopled by the Canadian [French] race." He was right about the catastrophe. The catastrophe was the American Revolution; its result was that Canada would no longer be wholly French.

The Loyalist settlers in Quebec, allying themselves with Montreal's British merchants, immediately, and strongly, took up the familiar demands for British institutions, British laws, and an elected assembly. They encouraged British administrators to revive the notion of assimilation of the Canadiens and to make Quebec into an English-speaking colony. The Montreal merchants intensified their pressure on the British government to repeal the Quebec Act and its provision for French civil law. Perceiving themselves responsible for the province's economic growth, they believed they were also entitled to assume political power. They wanted an elected assembly, preferably one controlled by the English-speaking minority, that would curb the governor's arbitrary power. The professional and merchant classes of the Canadiens also showed increasing interest in an elected assembly, leaving the seigneurs steadfastly opposed and preferring the status quo to a system that might see their tenants become their political equals. As for the ordinary habitants, it was assumed, then and later, by British officials that the issue should not concern them. One official wrote: "The Canadian Habitants are, I really believe, an industrious, peaceable and well-disposed people; but they are, from their want of education and extreme simplicity, liable to be misled by designing and artful men, and were they once made fully sensible of their own independence, the worst consequences might ensue."

THE CONSTITUTIONAL ACT, 1791

The British government's fix for Quebec was to reduce "dissensions and animosities" among two "classes of men [women were recognized politically in the colony, but only barely], differing in their prejudices and perhaps in their interests." It did this by separating them. The Constitutional Act, 1791 (or Canada Act) divided the Province of Quebec into Upper and Lower Canada. The French remained the majority in Lower Canada, the English-speaking Loyalists the majority in Upper Canada. The boundary line was the Ottawa River – except for a last jog around the farthest-west seigneury (a jog that ensured Montreal would be left in Lower Canada instead of being placed, as its British merchants passionately desired, in Upper Canada).

The act established identical institutions of governance in the two Canadas, designed to look like Britain's parliamentary model of sovereign, appointed House of Lords, and elected House of Commons. At the head of the colonial hierarchy was a governor-in-chief appointed by the British government and resident in Quebec City. For each colony, there was to be a lieutenant-governor, also appointed by the British government. Each lieutenant-governor had an appointed executive council to function as his private advisers (i.e., privy council). Each colony had a bicameral legislature consisting of an appointed legislative council and an elected House of Assembly. Appointments to the

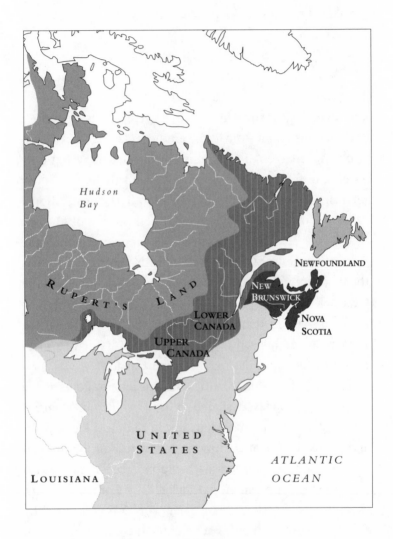

Constitutional Act, 1791

legislative council were for life, and the Constitutional Act went so far as to contemplate inherited membership from a British North American aristocracy, giving the King power to grant "hereditary titles of honour, rank or dignity."

The governors were to serve as the link between Imperial authority and local interests. Their assent was required for any bill passed by the colonial legislature to become law. They shared administrative and judicial responsibilities with their executive councils, which met approximately once a month to consider petitions or special favours, to issue regulations, and to approve grants and licences recommended by government departments. The elected assemblies could raise money through taxes for local expenditures, thus reducing the cost of the colonies to the Imperial treasury (the British government had not imposed taxes on its colonies since 1776). However, the Constitutional Act gave them less control over public funds than the legislatures of the former American colonies had enjoyed. The governor and his executive council were alone entitled to use the revenues from a vast expanse of Crown lands, giving them fiscal independence to do what they wanted. Another one-seventh of Crown lands in both provinces was set aside for the maintenance of the "Protestant clergy," meaning the Anglican Church. Both the governor and the appointed legislative council could veto legislation passed by the elected assembly, as could the British government.

The act said that the laws of the former Province of Quebec were to remain in force in both Upper and Lower Canada unless altered by their respective legislatures. This meant the continuance of French civil law in Lower Canada. The first act of the legislature of Upper Canada, in 1792, however, was to adopt (or "receive") English law for "all

matters of controversy relative to property and civil rights."
The privileges of the Roman Catholic Church remained in
force in Lower Canada. The oath of allegiance in both provinces was to the King as "lawful sovereign," not head of
the church.

As can be frequently observed about the British, what
they said they were doing was a distance removed from
what they did. They said they were giving the North
American colonies a system of governance identical to the
British Parliament at Westminster. They said that, with
Upper Canada, they were presenting the continent with a
model British society which Canadiens and Americans alike
would admire and perhaps even ask to join. In reality,
members of the British Parliament – both government and
opposition – were concerned less about actual conditions in
Canada than about American republicanism and French
democracy.[*] In reality, they created a system of governance
that could not possibly work.

Following the American Revolution, there was an emerging political view in Britain that colonies inevitably would
grow toward independence. In 1791 it remained a minority
view. The so-called mercantilist concept of empire still pre-
vailed: that colonies existed for the economic benefit of the
mother country, and their trade should therefore be controlled by Imperial laws, and their laws regulated by Imperial
legislators. The mercantilist concept led to the official

---

[*] The American Revolution had been completed in 1783, eight years
earlier. The French Revolution had begun in 1789 – two years earlier –
and, at precisely the same time as the Constitutional Act was being
debated in Westminster, the flight from the country of King Louis XVI
had been halted by a mob and he and his queen had been brought to
Paris and forced to accept a constitutional monarchy.

government view that revolution in America had been the product of too much democracy; therefore, less democracy was revolution's antidote. The government's intentions were clear: the Canadas were to become a North American bulwark against the presumptuous levelling tendencies of the age. John Graves Simcoe, the able and energetic first lieutenant-governor of Upper Canada, might boast that the Constitutional Act provided "no mutilated constitution but the very image and transcript of that of Great Britain." But it was a system modelled only superficially after Westminster. "We pretend to give Canada the same constitution as we ourselves live under," wrote a British minister. "All we can do is lay the foundation for the same constitution when increased population and time shall have made the Canadians ripe to receive it."

The elected assembly was the weakest part of the model. It could exert little control over public finances, and its legislative power was subject to a double check, from both the legislative council and the governor and his executive council. (It was as if, in modern context, the Senate, the governor general, and the prime minister and cabinet could veto any legislation passed by the Canadian House of Commons.) The notion of an appointed executive council to advise a governor was not new in colonial governance, but an appointed legislative council – patterned after the hereditary House of Lords – was. And while the British government's idea of a hereditary membership was soon forgotten (the notion of backwoods dukes pitching hay could not be taken seriously), the council's powers remained real: without its consent no measure passed by the House of Assembly could become law. Liberal reformers in Westminster ridiculed much of the Constitutional Act, but not this part. The brilliant Charles James Fox, speaking in Parliament, declared the best constitution to be one in which "monarchy, aristocracy and democracy [are] blended . . . nor could any government be a fit one for British subjects to live under, which did not contain its due weight of aristocracy . . . the proper poise of the constitution, the power that equalised and meliorated the powers of the two other extreme branches [sovereign and elected Commons], and gave stability and firmness to the whole."*

The Westminster politicians need not have worried. The coming of the Loyalists to the four remaining British North American provinces (formed, ironically, out of the old French Empire) had immensely strengthened the loyalty of these territories to Britain. (Even more important would be the flood of immigrants from the British Isles after the Napoleonic Wars ended in 1815.) This loyalism, with its emotional attachment to the Empire and its strong anti-American flavour, became one of the chief characteristics of English-speaking Canada in its formative years, a characteristic complicated, as always, by Canada's bicultural nature.

Fox did argue that the Constitutional Act's separation of English Loyalists and French Canadiens would prevent any possibility of union between the two. "The most desirable circumstance," he said, "was that the French and English inhabitants of Canada should unite and coalesce as it were into one body, and that the different distinctions of the people should be extinguished forever." Not so, said the prime minister, William Pitt the Younger: The best method of

---

* Fox's comments, of course, should be read in the context of what was going on at the time in France.

bringing them together was to separate them for a time. In any event, the British government assumed – wrongly – that the Canadiens, unaccustomed to an elected assembly, would probably not exercise much influence in it, leaving Lower Canada's affairs safely in the hands of its British governor and members of the British merchant elite, who would naturally be appointed to the legislative council.

With the imposition of the Constitutional Act, we can now glimpse the framework of modern Canada. There are separate provinces beneath a uniting superior government (the British government and its representatives, the governor general and lieutenant-governors). The provincial legislatures have constitutions "similar in principle" to that of Great Britain (the precise words of the British North America Act of 1867). Within their boundaries, the provinces have legislative jurisdiction over most local matters, in particular property and civil rights. (Provincial control over property rights was a direct result of the legal recognition of seigneurial land tenure.) The provinces have their own systems of civil law. Lower Canada has special laws and institutions reflecting the traditional customs of its French inhabitants.

REBELLION AGAINST THE FEW, 1791–1837
In the years between the Constitutional Act and Confederation, the primary forces shaping the Canadian state and its Constitution acquired full body: first, French–English conflict; second, Canadien nationalism; third, class struggle; fourth, a fight over who controlled government revenues; fifth, a complementary (and ethnically transcending) combination of inherent conservatism and loyalty to the Crown;

sixth, the aspirations of mercantile capitalists. Reaching critical mass in 1837, these forces produced rebellion, albeit of a rather Canadian nature: brief, bumbling, not too bloody, and largely disapproved of by the public. Rebellion, nevertheless, was what it took to draw the Imperial government's attention to the flaws in British North America's constitutional framework.

Modern Canadians are not inclined to think of their constitutional development in terms of class struggle – but, in the 1830s, that was precisely the dynamic in play. The Constitutional Act had created elective assemblies so powerless as to be little more than debating clubs. Power resided with the governor and with the men he appointed to the executive and legislative councils, men who held, and wished to protect, positions of power and influence in the community and who controlled the patronage and favours that the government could dispense.

In Upper Canada, the oligarchy was the Family Compact, so called because its members came from a small number of well-to-do and long-established families, often of Loyalist origin. They and their friends acquired vast tracts of land (Simcoe, seeking to create a landed aristocracy as was suggested in the Act, had given members of the executive and legislative councils between 1,200 and 2,000 hectares each and their children 480 hectares) which they sold at speculative prices, thus discouraging easy settlement. They also were the capitalists who controlled banks, who used public funds to build canals that enriched themselves and their associates (but who could not find the money to pay for roads and schools for frontier municipalities) and they were the judiciary and the senior clergy of the Anglican Church with its assertion of establishment and of entitlement to revenues from public lands. Writing in their defence in the late 1830s, Upper Canada's lieutenant-governor, Sir Francis (Galloping Head) Bond Head, wrote: "This 'family compact' is nothing more nor less than that 'social fabric' which characterizes every civilized community in the world. . . . [It] is composed of those members of its society who, either by their abilities and character have been honoured by the confidence of the executive government, or who, by their industry and intelligence, have amassed wealth. The party, I own, is comparatively a small one; but to put the multitude at the top and the few at the bottom is a radical reversion of the pyramid of society which every reflecting man must foresee can end only by its downfall." Thus, the constitutional struggle in Upper Canada was against the privileges of the few at the top. The remedy sought was control by the people over the executive, either by means of American-style democratic institutions of governance, with their separation of powers and checks and balances, or by British-style responsible government, which would require the governor to choose members of his executive council who had the support of the elective assembly.

In Lower Canada, the oligarchy was called the Château Clique, after the name of the governor's mansion, Château Saint-Louis. Some of its members came from the seigneurial class and senior ranks of the Roman Catholic clergy. Mostly, however, they were the familiar crowd of Montreal British merchants, variously described as English Canada's only aristocracy and the most "purposeful and assertive of all the Canadian social classes" who so effortlessly entrenched themselves around the governor.

The framers of the Constitutional Act had not expected their work would intensify French–English division; rather,

they hoped their grant of a representative assembly to
French Canadians would help transform or assimilate them.
They were wrong. The Quebec Act, by its special treatment
of the Canadiens, had made them conscious of their separate
position. The Constitutional Act was not contradictory but
complementary; by giving the French both a territorial base
and an elective assembly in Lower Canada, it protected
them from absorption and subordination. Many members
of the emerging French professional class found politics a
natural vehicle for their social ambitions. Espousing liberal,
democratic, and even republican ideals, they became champions of national cultural values and aspired to replace the
clergy and what French seigneurs were left (more than half
the seigneuries were in British hands by the early decades of
the nineteenth century) as leaders of French Canada. They
immediately won control of the Lower Canada Assembly
and established French on an equal footing with English
as its official languages. They took as their motto, "Our
Language, Our Institutions, Our Laws." Their leader, Louis-
Joseph Papineau, a lawyer and seigneur, was elected Speaker
of the Assembly in 1815 at age twenty-nine.

The Reform Party in Upper Canada and Parti canadien
(later Parti patriote) in Lower Canada made similar demands
for popular control over their provinces' executive government and finances. Reform had its *Seventh Report on
Grievances* written by William Lyon Mackenzie, first mayor
of Toronto. The Lower Canada Assembly passed its Ninety-
Two Resolutions. The demands were rejected by the British
government. Rebellion erupted by accident. Rioting broke
out in Montreal following a mass meeting of the Patriotes
on November 7, 1837. Believing his presence in the city

might lead to further trouble, Papineau decided to leave the city, an action the government interpreted as a move to spread the disturbances to the countryside. Attempts to arrest the Patriotes' leaders set off armed clashes. The rebellion in Upper Canada was precipitated by the events in Lower Canada. ("Up then, brave Canadians," exhorted Mackenzie. "Get ready your rifles and make short work of it.") Both uprisings were easily put down.

Modern Canadians, steeped in the mythology of the peaceful, law-abiding nature of their society, should reflect for a moment on what depth of provocation could lead the citizens of their country to armed rebellion.

In part it was the times. The documents from both Canadian assemblies refer to the achievements of the American and French revolutions. But, that being said, rebellion in Canada did not have popular support. The documents show that what the rebels desired was not an insurrection against the Crown or against the Imperial connection – against Britain's control over colonial trade, for example, which figured so prominently as a cause of rebellion in the American colonies. As one Upper Canadian Reformer wrote in 1824: "We like American liberty well, but greatly prefer British liberty. [As] British subjects, . . . we have sworn allegiance to a constitutional monarchy and we will die before we violate that oath." What did reflect the majority popular will in Lower and Upper Canada was the desire for the same constitutional guarantees enjoyed under responsible government by Britons, and for an end to the privileges of the wealthy and other elites – specifically the Anglican Church in Upper Canada and the domination of the British "mercantile aristocracy – the most abominable, the most pernicious of governments"[*] – over the French majority in Lower Canada.

The British government reacted to the rebellions by suspending the constitution of Lower (but not Upper) Canada – meaning Lower Canada no longer had an elected assembly – and by appointing John Lambton, Earl of Durham, one of the most advanced liberal reformers of the age, as governor general of British North America with a mandate to investigate and propose solutions for its troubles. Durham spent five months in the Canadas, but only two weeks in Upper Canada. He quit in a huff over a disagreement with the British Colonial Office and went home to write one of the most important documents of Canadian constitutional history, *Report on the Affairs of British North America*. Three of his recommendations are relevant to this book.

UNION OF THE CANADAS

Durham recommended that the Constitutional Act's division of the "Old Province of Quebec" be undone and that Upper and Lower Canada be reunited into one province. Durham shared the view of the colonial merchants: that the St. Lawrence waterway was a single geographic and economic unit – not divided by colonial boundaries – to which the future prosperity of the Canadas was linked; that a divided government made it difficult to co-ordinate plans for the waterway's development; and, in particular, that the French in their Assembly of Lower Canada should no longer be allowed to block what the Montreal merchants defined as economic expansion. Durham also accepted the

[*] *Le Canadien*, first newspaper in French Canada, 1806.

hoary British colonial policy toward Canada: the assimilation of the Canadiens. He called them, in his famous words, "a people with no literature and no history . . . an utterly uneducated and singularly inert population . . . destitute of all that can invigorate and elevate a people." In the context of his age and its intellectual assumptions, he was not (the argument has been made) being unjust: He believed in the superiority of British civilization and government and thought the French in a united Canada would be led naturally and gradually to give up their separate ways and be peacefully absorbed into a wholly British Canada. He wrote:

> It will be acknowledged by everyone who has observed the progress of Anglo-Saxon colonization in America, that sooner or later the English race was sure to predominate even numerically in Lower Canada, as they predominate already by their superior knowledge, energy, enterprise and wealth. The error, therefore, to which the present contest must be attributed [the political conflict in Lower Canada], is the vain endeavour to preserve a French-Canadian nationality in the midst of Anglo-American colonies and states. . . .
>
> It must henceforth be the first and steady purpose of the British government to establish an English population, with English laws and language . . . and to trust to none but a decidedly English legislature.

RESPONSIBLE GOVERNMENT

One of the merry oddities of Canadian history is that the most important constitutional recommendation credited to Durham – responsible government – may not have been invented when he proposed it. It existed in bits and pieces at the time he drew up his report, and certainly the concept was in some people's minds. But it had no concrete form or official recognition even in the mother of parliaments at Westminster and the idea of it existing in a colony sat very uncomfortably with London's imperial legislators.

In a system of fully responsible government, the colonial governor – acting as the sovereign would act in Parliament – would be compelled to choose as members of his executive council (analogous to a privy council or cabinet) only those persons who had the support of the elected assembly. He also would be compelled to accept their advice and assent to their legislation. What Durham recommended was something like that – although his report suggested the governor should still actively frame policy – and, in so doing, he created a new, and enormously important, notion of a divisible Crown, a notion that was to be essential thirty years later to the creation and function of a Canadian federal state. "Divisible Crown" meant that, at one and the same time, while a constitutional sovereign sitting in London was required to give assent to legislation passed by the elected House of Commons in Westminster, so in Canada a governor acting in the sovereign's name would be required to give assent to legislation passed by the elected colonial assembly. Needless to say, Durham's recommendation posed a conundrum: how could a single sovereign be required to give consent to what might be conflicting legislation emanating from two different authorities? Lord John Russell, the British colonial secretary, was in no doubt as to the answer. If the Empire were to be maintained, he said, the colonial governor and his executive council had to be responsible to the imperial government in London, not the colonial assembly.

DIVISION OF POWERS

Durham's solution to Russell's objections was to propose a division of powers, in which the colonial legislature would have constitutional jurisdiction over virtually all local matters while constitutional amendment, regulation of trade and foreign relations, and management of public lands would be reserved for the Imperial Parliament. Russell still did not accept the idea: "There are some cases of internal government in which the honour of the Crown or the faith of Parliament or the safety of the State are so seriously involved that it would not be possible for Her Majesty [Queen Victoria] to delegate her authority to a Ministry in a colony." Before another twenty years passed, the British did accept the notion, with seminal implications for one of the great constitutional debates of Canada: Was Confederation the creation of a federal state, with Imperial jurisdiction transferred from London to the government of the new nation in 1867, or was it no more than a pact between the French and the English?

THE UNITED PROVINCE OF CANADA, 1841–1867

The Act of Union, passed by the British government in 1840 and proclaimed in 1841, reunited Lower and Upper Canada into one colony with two sections, Canada East and Canada West. It was not the first but the second time the British had tried to undo the division of the colony effected by the Constitutional Act, 1791. It made the attempt in 1822, but dropped the idea in the face of a storm of opposition from the French Canadians. This time, the politicians of Upper Canada were persuaded to accept it, and the politicians of Lower Canada, with its constitution suspended, simply had it imposed on them. "We give Lower Canada no choice," said Lord John Russell.

The Act of Union:

• Continued to provide Canada with a framework of governance that looked like Britain's. There was a governor, an appointed executive council, a legislative council whose members were appointed for life, and an elective assembly. As before, the governor, in the sovereign's name, could assent to bills, withhold assent, or "reserve" bills for consideration by the Imperial Parliament (which could disallow colonial legislation). There was no provision in the act for responsible government;

• Decreed that English would be the only language of official records and proceedings of the legislative council and legislative assembly;

• Provided for an equal number of elected representatives – forty-two – from each section of the united province. This was designed to benefit Canada West, which had a smaller population than Canada East. It backfired within a few years, when the population of Canada West passed that of Canada East;

• Continued to allow for French civil law in Canada East, but it was a provision that could be altered by act or ordinance of the new legislature – that is, it was not constitutionally protected;

• Established a single consolidated revenue fund, with

the result that Canada West's substantial debt – the result of its canal-building program – was offloaded onto debt-free Canada East;

- Finally, although, in theory, the governor could select French Canadians for his executive council, in practice they were barred.

This was a policy patently designed to bring about the cultural demise of Canada's French-speaking population. Charles Buller, who had been secretary to Durham, wrote: "We have put down their rebellion, destroyed their nationality and, in doing this, reduced them to a miserable state of social subjection." Charles Poulett Thomson, Baron Sydenham, who followed Durham as governor general, saw to it that the capital was located at Kingston, in English-speaking Canada. "A capital somewhere in Upper Canada would be good for French-speaking members," he said, "because it would instill English ideas into their minds [and] destroy the immediate influence upon their actions of the host of little lawyers, notaries and doctors." At the union's formal inauguration, Pierre-Joseph-Olivier Chauveau, destined to become the first post-Confederation premier of Quebec, proclaimed: "Today a weeping people is beaten, tomorrow a people will be up in arms; today the forfeit, tomorrow the vengeance."* The united province ran a quarter-century course, from political paralysis to oblivion.

It was a transition period, happily brief, and, while it lasted, six important things happened:

---

* The twentieth-century Quebec nationalist historian Maurice Séguin has called the Act of Union "the second Conquest."

1. The united colony did turn out to be a more efficient economic unit than the formerly divided Upper and Lower Canada.

2. Responsible government did occur after 1848, with the election of a new Liberal government in Imperial Britain and the arrival, as colonial secretary, of Earl Grey who decided to give Durham's recommendations a fair trial.

3. Instead of the assimilation the French feared and Westminster intended, English-Canadian politicians discovered they could not assemble a majority to govern the country without involving the French.* Joint (English-French) premierships became common during the union's lifetime.

4. Once responsible government was established, French-speaking representatives who had the support of the elected assembly to form a government became members of the executive council as a matter of course.

5. Although the act prescribed English as the only official language and expressly banished French from official government use, no restriction was placed on French as a language of translation or debate. Indeed, as a matter of practice both languages were used in debate from the very first session, and the act was amended in 1848 to remove the prohibition on French. (The act also was amended to make appointments to the legislative council

---

* "In fact, the great majority of the French in the assembly combined into one group, while English-Canadians were divided into various groups of Tories and Reformers. The English-speaking majority could not assert its total strength. Under responsible government, as a result, any cabinet had to be a loose alliance of French and English, representing equally the English-controlled Canada West and French-controlled Canada East," as J.M.S. Careless pointed out in *Canada: A Story of Challenge*.

for eight years, rather than life – a change curiously undone when the Senate replaced the council in 1867.) 6. The notion of division of powers was accepted. In 1852, Earl Grey wrote that the imperial government in London was ready to let the colonies govern their internal affairs, and to reserve for itself that jurisdiction which "is indispensable either for the purpose of preventing any one Colony from adopting measures injurious to another, or to the Empire at large, or else for the promotion of the internal good government of the Colonies, by assisting the inhabitants to govern themselves." *

Responsible government slowly made its mark elsewhere in British North America – with less noise and sometimes with less permanence. In Nova Scotia, responsible government was achieved in 1848, largely through the efforts of Joseph Howe, who conducted the colony's equivalent of the 1837 rebellions in Upper and Lower Canada. New Brunswick and Prince Edward Island, with sparse populations and no major political centres equivalent to Halifax,

---

* The political scientist Robert McGregor Dawson noted in *The Government of Canada*: "Responsible government within the Empire, as Durham and others clearly realized, could only be conceded at that time if it was placed squarely upon a separation of Imperial and local affairs. . . . The line of demarcation . . . proved in the event to be neither clearcut nor obvious, and the desire for more and more autonomy began immediately to widen the local area and narrow that which had been reserved in general terms for the Imperial authorities. . . . These developments were eventually to affect many aspects of Canadian government, and they did not reach their logical destination until 1926 and 1931 when the full equality of Great Britain and the Dominions [at the time, Canada, Australia, New Zealand, South Africa, Ireland and Newfoundland] was formally declared."

won responsible government – in 1848 and 1851 respectively –
largely without asking for it. Newfoundland won responsible government in 1855 but lost it again in 1934 when economic collapse led to the colony being ruled directly by
Britain, until a majority of its people voted to join Canada
in 1949. The other pre-Confederation British Crown colony
– British Columbia – did not acquire responsible government until it became a Canadian province in 1871.

Confederation of the British North American provinces,
the great climacteric of Canadian history, was mooted almost
from the moment the American colonies won independence
in 1783. Carleton had advocated it. Durham advocated it.
The establishment of responsible government along with
the simultaneous abandonment by Britain of mercantile
empire bestowed on the idea an almost unstoppable impe-
tus and lighted the fire beneath the bottoms of Canadian
legislators. The one gave the British provinces and territories
a muscular political preparation for the venture while the
other, which cast the provinces economically adrift from
Britain, forced them to seek their own economic solutions.
"The Confederation movement," historian P.B. Waite has
written, "followed Newton's first law of motion: all bodies
continue in a state of rest or of uniform motion unless
compelled by some force to change their state."

THE SPRINT TO CONFEDERATION, 1864–1867
English-French differences in the union legislature became
so chronically acrimonious in the late 1850s and early 1860s
that government was paralysed. Political agreement eluded
the politicians on most pressing decisions, such as the need
to strengthen the militia at a time when relations with the

United States threatened to lead to war. The constitutional requirement of equal representation from the two sections had – from the moment Canada West's population surpassed that of Canada East in 1851 – become a large thorn in the side of the Canada West politicians. Measures "imposed" on one section of the country by a majority made up of representatives of the other section caused bitterness. For example, while only a minority of representatives from Canada West voted in favour of the 1863 Scott Act, which gave added privileges to Roman Catholic schools in Canada West, it was adopted because of substantial support from the largest French bloc in the legislature, the *bleus*. George Brown, editor and founder of the *Globe* newspaper and leader of the legislature's Clear Grit Reform Party, summed up matters this way: "We have two races, two languages, two systems of religious belief, two systems of everything, so that it has become almost impossible that, without sacrificing their principles, the public men of both sections could come together in the same government. The difficulties have gone on increasing every year."

Few wanted to turn back the clock to 1791 and again set the two Canadas on their separate ways. Brown and other – though by no means all – members wanted a federal union to replace the United Province's legislative union, with most matters left to local legislatures. To maintain a governing majority, co-premiers John A. Macdonald and Etienne-Paschal Taché in June, 1864, reluctantly accepted George Brown's three conditions for entering what has become known as "The Great Coalition." Brown's conditions: that the coalition government work toward a federation of all the British North American colonies and, failing this, at least a federation of the two Canadas; that there be elected representation according to population, thus ending the old system of equal sectional representation, and that the great Northwest be incorporated into the federation. The premiers of the three Maritime provinces had agreed to meet to discuss Maritime union. Suddenly, members of the Canadian government asked permission to attend. The meeting was set for September 1, 1864, in Charlottetown. The march to Confederation began.

CHAPTER 2

THE VISION OF THE FATHERS

Thus the first Dominion Day, celebrated with church services, parades, band music, picnics and fireworks from Halifax to Sarnia, was a day rather of beginning than of ending; of endeavours planned, rather than achievements reviewed. Much as had been done already, it was only that an undertaking greater still might be attempted.
— W.L. Morton, *The Kingdom of Canada*

THE FEDERAL DOMINION OF CANADA began life on July 1, 1867, with a new capital, a central government, four provinces,* and a written constitution, the British North America Act. In all the debate, dispute, and discord on the nature of the country that has occurred since then, there is consensus on what the original vision was. The politicians who created what they called "Confederation" on the northern half of the North American continent intended it should have a strong central government to which the provinces, the constituent parts, would be subordinate. Only reluctantly had the first prime minister, John A. Macdonald, agreed to a federation of any sort (although federation was

---

* The English common-law provinces of Ontario, Nova Scotia, and New Brunswick, and the French Civil Code province of Quebec.

probably all that Quebec and the two Atlantic colonies would accept).

The Fathers of Confederation had examined the one other model of federalism in existence at that time – that of the United States, still devastated by civil war – and had rejected it. In their view, the lesson from war between the states was that the framers of the U.S. Constitution had erred in giving individual states too much power and the central government too little. Thus, in that canon of political dreams and thought that enriches our history as the *Confederation Debates*, we find Sir John A. saying: "In framing the Constitution, care should be taken to avoid the mistakes and weaknesses of the U.S. system, the primary error of which was the reservation to the different states of all powers not delegated to the General [Federal] Government. We must reverse this process by establishing a strong central government to which shall belong all powers not specifically conferred on the provinces." *The reverse of the U.S. model.* Canada's Constitution not only would divide legislative responsibilities between the federal and provincial governments so that the muscle remained at the centre, it would assign to the central government all powers not specifically mentioned in the Constitution – known in constitutionalese as the "residual power." Here is Macdonald:

> Ever since the [American] union was formed the difficulty of what is called 'State Rights' has existed, and this had much to do in bringing on the present unhappy war in the U.S. They commenced, in fact, at the wrong end. They declared by their Constitution that each state was a sovereignty in itself, and that all powers incident to a sovereignty belonged to each

state, except those powers which, by the Constitution, were conferred upon the General Government and Congress. Here we have adopted a different system. We have strengthened the General Government. We have given the General Government all the great subjects of legislation. We have conferred on them, not only specifically and in detail, all the powers which are incident to sovereignty, but we have expressly declared that all subjects of general interest not distinctly and exclusively conferred upon the local governments and local legislatures, shall be conferred upon the General Government and Legislature. We have thus avoided that great source of weakness which has been the cause of the disruption of the United States.

Except that is not what happened. One of the great themes of Canadian constitutional history is how the 1867 vision of the Fathers of Confederation came to be so thoroughly thwarted so that, today, Canada is regarded by constitutional scholars as the most decentralized nation in the world. Moreover, despite that current degree of decentralization, most of the nation's political, academic, and journalistic elites insist that the central government must abandon even more powers in the interests of both national unity and enhanced efficiency. It is as if to say that we have so little in common as Canadians, share so few values and interests, that we can continue to exist as a national society only if there is nothing to bind us together. That is not the way we started out.

THE DIVISION OF POWERS

Federalism in 1867 was an old idea with old problems described by inexact labels. Canada at birth was called a "confederation," a misnomer arbitrarily applied to what the Fathers envisioned.

"Confederation" means a loose association of constituent states or provinces in which the central government functions only with the co-operation and consent of the provincial governments and is dependent upon them for such things as money and armies. For example, the American colonies established a "confederation" in 1777 because the central government was merely a delegate of the states. In contrast, as we know from both the British North America Act* and the words of the Fathers of Confederation, the Canadian central government was assigned "all the great subjects of legislation . . . all the powers which are incident [accessories] to sovereignty [and] . . . all subjects of general interest not distinctly and exclusively conferred upon the local governments and local legislatures [i.e., the residual power]."

The formula was this: to the general (i.e., central, federal, Dominion) government all matters of common interest to the whole country; to the provincial governments all matters of local interest within their respective territories. And to the Dominion government as well went the residual (or general) power – that is, the power to legislate on anything left over, or unthought of, after everything else had been assigned. The residual power was contained in that best-known, dryly prosaic phrase of Canada's Constitution,

---

* Since 1982 titled "The Constitution Act, 1867." For clarity and simplicity, we refer to it as the BNA Act unless quoting from post-1982 documents and speeches.

"to make Laws for the Peace, Order and good Government"
– POGG, for short – found in the preamble to the BNA Act's
Section 91 ("Powers of the Parliament").* The full preamble
reads as follows:

> It shall be lawful for the Queen by and with the Advice
> and Consent of the Senate and House of Commons, to
> make Laws for the Peace, Order and good Government
> of Canada, in relation to all Matters not coming within
> the Classes of Subjects by this Act assigned exclusively
> to the Legislatures of the Provinces; and *for greater
> Certainty* [emphasis ours], but not so as to restrict the
> Generality of the foregoing Terms of this Section, it
> is hereby declared that (notwithstanding anything
> in this Act) the exclusive Legislative Authority of the
> Parliament of Canada extends to all Matters coming
> within the Classes of Subjects next hereinafter enu-
> merated . . . [and Section 91 goes on to give the twenty-
> nine – now thirty-one – enumerated areas where the
> federal government had jurisdiction].

As events turned out, the Constitution's centralist framers
need not have written in the twenty-nine enumerations
and, indeed, they almost certainly would have been spared
much later grief if they hadn't. The language of Section 91
is precise: the Dominion government could exercise the
POGG power to legislate for all matters not assigned exclusively to the provinces, and the twenty-nine enumerations

---

* Sections 91 and 92 specify the areas in which, respectively, the federal
Parliament and the provincial legislatures are constitutionally authorized – or "competent" – to legislate.

in Section 91 were intended *not* as a finite list of federal areas of jurisdiction, but as an *illustration* ("for greater certainty") of where the POGG power could be applied.

There was no doubt in the Fathers' minds why the broad power was assigned to the central government: it was for the business of running a country. The aim was to facilitate national economic development precisely by ridding the new country of the competitive obstacles of the pre-Confederation colonies. Certainly in the minds of many of the new country's inhabitants, Canada was created by mercantile capitalists and railway owners who needed a central administration from which to settle and exploit the country. "Questions of commerce, of international communication, and all matters of general interest," said George-Étienne Cartier, leader of the French-Canadian group supporting Confederation, "would be discussed and determined in the General Legislature. . . ." As for French-Canadian supporters specifically, Confederation was that step toward a country where, by history and constitution, their language, law, and religion would be secured.

All the major economic powers were assigned to the Dominion government – trade and commerce, agriculture and immigration (these last two shared, with federal paramountcy), fishing, navigation and shipping, railways and canals, which in total covered most economic activity and most workers in the nineteenth-century country. Moreover, "works" (economic facilities) falling totally within any one provincial jurisdiction could be declared a Dominion responsibility under the Constitution by a simple declaration from Parliament that they existed "for the general advantage of Canada," a provision used many times by the federal government in respect of local railways, but also to assert federal regulation over grain elevators and the grain trade in the late 1960s. Similarly, while the provinces were given the ownership of their natural resources (lands, mines, forests, and waterpower), once these were developed and their products entered the stream of "trade and commerce using interprovincial services" they fell under federal jurisdiction.

Banks, legal tender, interest, weights and measures, customs and excise (the last two taken away from the provinces at the time of Confederation in return for the Dominion government assuming their public debt) were all federal. Provincial tariffs were prohibited. The federal government was given unlimited power to tax while the provinces were restricted to direct taxation (such as sales tax).

Perhaps nothing illustrated more clearly the Fathers' vision of Canada than the BNA Act's Section 94. Unburdened of its fusty Victorian legal draftsmanship, Section 94 authorized the Dominion government to make uniform laws for property and civil rights in the three common-law provinces. This amounted to authorization for the federal Parliament to intrude into provincial jurisdiction, should those provinces agree, with the precise aim of strengthening the union. Constitutional scholar F.R. Scott wrote in 1942:

The purpose of the section, if we leave aside for the moment its geographical applicability, is quite clear. None of the writers who have considered it have been in any doubt about it. Section 92 left the subject of "Property and Civil Rights in the province" within the exclusive jurisdiction of provincial legislatures. If the Act had stopped there, Canada would have been divided into watertight compartments which it would have been impossible to break down without going through the difficult process of amending the Constitution itself. The law which established federalism [the BNA Act] would itself have been an obstacle in the way of greater national unity should the desire for unity ever arise.

Now the last thing the Fathers of Confederation wished to do was to prevent Canadians from becoming united. *They did not believe, and still less provided, that the divisions of their day would be perpetual* [emphasis ours]. The purpose of Confederation was to bring greater union, and to eradicate the exaggerated provincialism which was holding back all sections of British North America in 1867. While for various and good reasons a federation and not a legislative union was all that could be agreed upon, it was clearly understood and intended by the framers of the Act that, outside Quebec, an easy way should be left open for an even closer integration of the provinces than was provided at the beginning by the Act itself. . . . Quebec was excluded from this provision, because the guaranteeing of her control over her basic civil laws was looked upon as part of the racial agreement implicit in the Constitution.

Of course, opponents of Confederation objected to the 1867 division of powers precisely on the grounds of excessive centralization. For example, Antoine-Aimé Dorion, leader of the radical liberals, or Rouges, declared: "The Confederation I advocated was a real confederation, giving the largest powers to the local governments, and merely a delegated authority to the General Government – in that respect differing *in toto* from the one now proposed, which gives all the power to the central and reserves for the local governments the smallest possible amount of freedom of action." He was correct. The provinces were granted only a moderate list of powers, those being essentially of a local or private nature. Even some non-economic powers, which under the American Constitution had been assigned to the states – for example, criminal law, marriage, and divorce – were given to Canada's Dominion government.

The great authority on Canadian governance, McGregor Dawson, has written: "The provinces [under the BNA Act] were to be inferior bodies. . . . Even the sketchy records of the contemporary discussions which have come down to us contain scattered references to 'municipal councils on a large scale,' 'local municipal parliaments,' and the like, while the provincial legislatures are repeatedly described as a 'subordinate,' 'minor,' and 'inferior' bodies."

The Dominion government was given power to appoint and remove the lieutenant-governor in each province, thereby assuming the role that prior to Confederation had been occupied by the British Imperial government in relation to the administration of British North America's individual colonies. No provincial bill could become law without the assent of the federally appointed lieutenant-governor. Ottawa also could order that a provincial bill be "reserved" by the lieutenant-governor, and the governor general could disallow or set aside any provincial law within a year of its passage – powers which, until the 1940s, were used with some frequency (as Macdonald, in an 1868 memorandum, had proclaimed would be the case). Although the federal powers of disallowance and reservation for provincial legislation still exist in the Constitution, they have fallen into disuse, and lieutenant-governors today act only on the advice of their respective provincial governments.

Finally, in the event of conflict between a valid federal law and a valid provincial law, where the Constitution said the two orders of government possessed concurrent jurisdiction (agriculture and immigration), the federal law would always prevail.

PARLIAMENTARY GOVERNMENT: RIGHTS OR NO RIGHTS?

Although the Fathers of Confederation opted for a federal state rather than a legislative union (a unitary state like the United Kingdom), they nonetheless preserved the machinery of parliamentary government. The BNA Act, in its preamble, prescribed that the new Dominion was to have a constitution "similar in principle to that of the United Kingdom," the central feature of which is parliamentary sovereignty. The Fathers simply created parliamentary government at two levels (Dominion and provincial), wrote a constitution that specified which level of government would do what things, and imported British constitutional conventions and traditions for just about everything else – for example, civil rights.

Macdonald called the American presidential system a "great evil." "The President," he said, "is the leader of a Party, and obliged to protect the rights of a majority. Under the British Constitution, with the people having always the power in their own hands [with supreme executive authority vested in the constitutional sovereign, who represents all the people] and with the responsibility of a Ministry to Parliament, we are free from such despotism." Of course, since then the growth and expansion of cabinet authority in Canada – government by ministerial fiat and regulation without recourse to Parliament – have given rise to similar accusations of "despotism." Nevertheless, in 1867 British parliamentary government was considered superior to the presidential system. The new Dominion government – with provincial governments following a similar form – consisted of a group of ministers of the Crown made up of the members of the dominant party of the Lower House (the elected House of Commons) under the leadership of a prime minister. The ministry, or cabinet, advised the Crown upon the exercise of its legislative powers and assumed responsibility for all its public actions.

The fact remained that the BNA Act had no specific mention (or "enumeration") of civil rights and liberties; no explicit reference to freedom of religion, speech, the press, and assembly; and no bill of rights comparable to the first ten amendments of the U.S. Constitution. But by importing into the BNA Act "a Constitution similar in principle to that of the United Kingdom," the framers thought they were constitutionalizing the essential concepts of popular government such as liberty of speech, due process of law, free elections, all considered sacred by tradition in the common law (the chief doctrine of which is that a person is free to do anything not positively prohibited). Maybe the framers were right, maybe they were not. The Supreme Court of Canada in the 1930s declared that the BNA Act did contain an "implied bill of rights"* – but many constitutional scholars have pointed out that parliamentary sovereignty, or supremacy, means just that: it invests Parliament with the authority to abolish anything, including civil rights, unless it is constitutionally declared to be beyond the reach of

---

* The 1938 *Alberta Press* case

legislative encroachment. (And, to that end, the BNA Act
contained provisions for annual sessions of Parliament, a
maximum of five years between elections, representation by
population, and a more or less independent judiciary.)

Initially, in Canada, questions about the protection of
rights were framed in the context of which level of government – federal or provincial – had jurisdiction, although
this was not always useful. In 1903, for example, the British
Judicial Committee of the Privy Council struck down
Ontario's Lord's Day Act. This, one would have thought,
was a matter falling under the definition of "Property and
Civil Rights in the Province" or of "a merely local or private
Nature in the Province," and therefore within provincial
jurisdiction under Section 92 of the BNA Act, but according
to the committee the prohibition of work on Sundays was
a "criminal law" within exclusive federal jurisdiction. The
Dominion Parliament subsequently enacted the federal
Lord's Day Act of 1906 with what may have been the first
provincial "opting out" provision in Canadian history.
The federal act stood for eighty years until it was declared
constitutionally inconsistent with the Charter of Rights
and Freedoms.

MINORITY RIGHTS
While the Fathers were a bit at sea on the general notion of
civil rights, they clearly had in mind the concept of minority rights. The BNA Act does place some absolute limitations on the principle of parliamentary sovereignty, and
these exist precisely to guarantee certain minority rights.
Section 93 of the BNA Act guaranteed separate denominational schools, a clause demanded by English Protestants in

Quebec, who feared they would be outnumbered and over-powered by French Roman Catholics. Section 133 protected the use of French and English in Parliament and the Quebec Legislature, and in the federal and Quebec courts. Quebec's Civil Code was protected both by the enumeration of "property and civil rights" as an exclusive provincial responsibility under Section 92, and by Section 94, which excluded Quebec from the authority granted to the Dominion Parliament – with approval from the common-law provinces – to legislate uniformity of court procedures and provincial laws relating to property and civil rights. Furthermore, the use of the French language in the legislature and courts was extended in 1870 to the new province of Manitoba, and in 1877 to the whole of the North-West Territories, from which Manitoba had been carved.[*]

Thus we see a Constitution which from the beginning fixed minimum guarantees for Canada's French-speaking minority and, within ten years, extended those guarantees to new parts of the Dominion. The Fathers of Confederation did not look upon the 1867 guarantees as a maximum but as a starting point. "The use of the French language," Macdonald said in the *Confederation Debates*, "should form one of the principles upon which Confederation should be established." The wording of Section 93 makes clear, among other things, that the Dominion government "may make remedial laws" if any provincial legislation respecting

---

[*] The North-West Territories included land purchased by Canada from the Hudson's Bay Company under the 1870 acquisition of Rupert's Land and North-Western Territory. It was, at the outset, governed by a federally appointed lieutenant-governor and council, comparable to earlier colonial governments.

education unconstitutionally restricts the rights of "denominational [religious]" minorities. Added to the Dominion's authority to disallow provincial legislation, the Constitution undoubtedly was intended to protect minorities (English Protestants in Quebec, French Roman Catholics outside Quebec) from discriminatory acts by the provinces. "We shall be able to protect the minority by having a strong central government," said Macdonald. A nice, even a prescient, thought. Since 1867, attacks on minorities, specifically their educational and linguistic rights, have nearly all come from provincial legislatures. Notwithstanding Canada's historical experience and the Fathers' intentions, those attacks illustrate that the 1867 Constitution's protections were fragile.

In 1890, the Manitoba legislature repealed the section of its provincial constitution – created by its union with Canada – which made French an official language. The North-West Territories had been granted an elective assembly in 1888 and, in 1891, the assembly was permitted by the Dominion government to decide for itself on the status of French. The following year it abolished the use of French in legislature debates. Saskatchewan and Alberta were created out of the territory in 1905 with only very limited provisions for Roman Catholic schools and the use of the French language – provisions which largely disappeared in 1918. Ontario in 1913 limited the use of French as a language of instruction in schools.

What we see here is that Confederation itself, with its centralized powers, did not pose a threat to the minority rights. Indeed, most French Canadians saw Confederation both as a protection against the threat of U.S. annexation and as a liberation from British colonialism – with language guarantees in the central government and constitutional protection for their civil law in Quebec. While there is no doubt that French Canadians, then as now, wanted to preserve their identity, in 1867 Confederation appeared as a realistic, pragmatic instrument for that very objective.

THE COMPACT THEORY OF CONFEDERATION

Every action ultimately breeds reaction. The long presence of the centralist Macdonald at the helm of national government (1867–73, 1878–91) undoubtedly fuelled the advance of the provincialist "compact theory" of Confederation – the idea that Confederation, rather than creating a new and sovereign nation, was in reality no more than a "treaty" or "pact" among the original provinces, or, conversely, between the two original colonizing groups, French and English. In support of this is cited language used by some of the participants in the Confederation Debates. The theory holds that, as a treaty, the act could only be altered or amended by the unanimous consent of Ottawa and the provinces, a notion that then, as now, ignores the fact that the BNA Act was not an agreement but a statute of a superior legislature (the British Parliament) and that it was never ratified by any formal act of the constituent "partners" (which is to say, the pre-1867 colonial legislatures). In the conclusion of McGregor Dawson: "The [compact] theory, while plausible, is constructed on sheer invention which has been subsequently propped up by an occasional precedent. It has no legal foundation; it has no historical foundation."

In words resonating eerily with Canada's situation today, political scientist and one-time federal Cabinet minister Norman McLeod Rogers wrote in 1931:

It [the compact theory] would mean that Canada
would be taking a deliberate step toward greater rigid-
ity in its constitutional arrangements when the whole
trend of modern economic life is emphasizing the vital
importance of flexibility in a rapidly changing world.
It would arrest the growth and hamper the expression
of the national idea in Canada.

Yet the theory has become the basis for most Quebec
nationalists' arguments for either constitutionally entrenched
"special status" and "distinct society" or complete separation. To a lesser but not insignificant degree, it underlies the
persistent claims made for greater autonomy by other
provinces.

The theory's historical roots, according to the Quebec
historian and nationalist icon Lionel Groulx, are to be
found in the Quebec Act of 1774 and the Constitutional
Act of 1791. Groulx says the first guaranteed the survival of
French Canadians and the second guaranteed the survival
of French Canada – together creating a distinct province
with an ethnic base and "a renewed conservation of the
French fact in Canada." Quebec, therefore, can never be
labelled one province of four (as it was in 1867) or, today,
one province of ten. And its people deserve – on the authority of historical continuum – special powers to ensure their
equality with the inhabitants of the rest of Canada.

As noted above, Quebec's provincialists have never been
alone in seizing on the theory for their own ends. A mere
twenty years after Confederation, Premiers Honoré Mercier
of Quebec and Oliver Mowat of Ontario met in Quebec
City with their counterparts from New Brunswick, Nova
Scotia, and Manitoba to promote "provincial rights" against

what they declared to be an encroaching federal government. They asserted the right of the provinces to initiate amendments to the BNA Act independently of the Dominion Parliament, rejected the federal constitutional power to reserve or disallow provincial legislation, demanded that the provinces (rather than only the Dominion executive) be given the power to appoint senators, and asked for greater financial autonomy within their provincial jurisdictions. A familiar refrain. Macdonald portrayed them as "malcontents" and as Liberals confronting their political opponents in Ottawa for political reasons.[*] He may have had a point. Mowat, the Father of Provincial Rights, who had articled as a law student with Macdonald, was a politician not yoked to the limitations of consistency: at the 1864 Quebec Conference setting the framework for Confederation, he had introduced the successful resolution on federal disallowance of provincial bills – the very measure which he now so vehemently opposed.

Five months later, the Toronto *Globe* set out the compact theory succinctly:

> The Confederation has its origin in a bargain between certain provinces, in which bargain the Provinces agree to unite for certain purposes and to separate or continue separated for others. . . . The Dominion was the creation of these provinces. . . . The Dominion, being nonexistent at the time the bargain was made, was plainly not a party to the bargain. It cannot, then,

---

[*] The governments of Ontario, Quebec, Nova Scotia, and New Brunswick were all Liberal. Manitoba's John Norquay administration called itself non-partisan.

be a party to a revision of the bargain. The power to revise the created body must be in the hands of those who created that body.

One might ask why, when delegates to the Confederation conferences in Charlottetown and Quebec City had so enthusiastically endorsed the framework of the country later written into the BNA Act, had so much powerful opposition developed around it, and so soon?

There were reasons: The economic rationale in 1867 for a strong central government eroded during the intermittent hard times that persisted in Canada through Confederation's first thirty years. The threat of American invasion and annexation had been removed from the stage. The addition of five (eventually six) more provinces to the original four made the country more geographically diverse and stimulated resentment of central control.

This was particularly true in the case of Manitoba, which achieved provincial status in 1870 largely because of political action by Louis Riel and his Métis National Committee.* Angered by the Dominion government's intentions to annex the vast North-West Territories (of which Manitoba was a part) from the Hudson's Bay Co. without regard to the wishes or rights of the local population, Riel and his supporters in 1869 blocked the arrival of

---

* British Columbia joined Canada by imperial order-in-council in 1871. Prince Edward Island followed in 1873. In 1880, the remaining British possessions in the north and west of the continent were added as the North-West Territories. The North-West Territories were further divided into the Yukon Territory in 1898, and Alberta and Saskatchewan in 1905, all by Dominion statute. Newfoundland and Labrador were admitted into Confederation in 1949 following a referendum.

the new territorial lieutenant-governor sent from Canada, halted the work of Canadian survey crews, and seized the main HBC post of Upper Fort Garry (near to the site of Winnipeg). They formed a provisional government which forced the Dominion government to negotiate terms of entry into Confederation for the territory's Red River Colony (the original Manitoba) – terms which included special constitutional rights for Métis and the French language.

(In 1885 Riel took on a leadership role in the North-West Rebellion, sparked by political and economic discontent among Métis and Indians. The rebellion was suppressed after two months of fighting and Riel – one-eighth Indian and seven-eighths French – was convicted of treason for which the automatic penalty was death. The federal government refused to commute his sentence and, in the face of overwhelming opposition from Quebec, ordered him hanged, thus turning him into an immortal symbol of the English-French struggle.)

That support for the "compact theory" is often voiced most strongly in Quebec may also be a result of the different motivations French Canadians had when they entered Confederation. F.R. Scott pointed out that, for Quebec, the entry into Confederation provided autonomy which it had not known previously. For Quebec, Confederation represented a partial escape from London's Imperial control and the 1841 union, and greater autonomy at home, while for the other provinces Confederation represented either the status quo (vis-à-vis a superior legislature – London replaced by Ottawa) or an acceptance of a measure of centralized control. "It is small wonder," wrote Scott, "that Quebec has always insisted most strongly that the constitution was designed to secure autonomy to the provinces.

This was peculiarly her experience." Yet, it is a historical fact that protections for French law and language, as well as the Roman Catholic religion, were firmly established and, indeed, expanded *before* Confederation. Between 1763 and 1867, under governments controlled by British Protestants, Canada's Roman Catholics were granted full political rights (at a time when they were limited in Britain).

The proponents of the compact theory ignore that the Dominion Parliament was the creation and heir *not* of the provinces, but of the Imperial Parliament in London. If there was any "compact" at the time of Confederation, writes F.R. Scott, "it was an agreement on all sides that the 'supreme authority,' the parliament of Westminster, would transfer its sovereignty to the new federal government for all national purposes in Canada, leaving to the former provinces a field of independent local activity, but shorn of a great part of the freedom they had possessed under the earlier constitutions."

The purpose of Confederation was to end the union of 1841 and unite the British North American colonies in a federal state: that is to say, to take away from local governments many of their existing powers and to place over them a new national government endowed with a wide general jurisdiction extending territorially to the whole country.

ASYMMETRY AND SPECIAL STATUS

Advocates of the compact theory are also attracted to the constitutional notions of asymmetry and special status. These notions imply that in 1867 some provincial governments (and, in subsequent years, other provinces as they joined the union) were given powers different from others. Thus, goes the argument, historical authority today exists for altering the Constitution to provide individual provinces with special powers which others do not enjoy. In reality, this means transferring powers from the federal government to particular provinces.

With some minor exceptions, this argument, too, is historically inaccurate. At the time of Confederation – and in subsequent years – no special political or legislative privileges were granted to Quebec or to any other province in relation to the distribution of powers between federal and provincial governments. Legislatively, they were the same. And while they are not perfectly equal, writes constitutional scholar Peter Hogg, "the differences are not so marked as to justify the description 'special status' for any province."

For example, Section 133 of the BNA Act guarantees that both French and English may be used in the legislature and courts of Quebec, and the Terms of Union under which Manitoba entered Confederation contain the same guarantee. (The Constitution Act, 1982, extends even broader language and education protections to New Brunswick's linguistic groups.) The point to be made is that these provisions merely protect French- and English-speaking minorities in the provinces to which they apply. They do not give special legislative status to any province.

Section 94 (which has never been used) allowed the Dominion Parliament to make uniform laws for "property and civil rights" for the three common-law provinces at the time of Confederation, but not for Quebec. The purpose here was not in any way to exclude Quebec, or to divide the country into two parts, but to honour the constitutional protection of Quebec's civil law – a protection existing since 1774 – by prohibiting the Quebec legislature from delegating to Ottawa jurisdiction over property and civil rights.

For the same reason, the Constitution stated that federally appointed judges in Quebec had to be appointed from the Quebec bar. The protection of Quebec's civil law in itself did not represent special status; it had no impact on the division of powers between federal and provincial governments, nor did it give Quebec larger powers than those exercised by the other provinces.

Following 1867, each of the other six provinces entered Confederation under its own Terms of Union, each under slightly different circumstances. British Columbia, for example, was guaranteed the completion of the transcontinental railway; Prince Edward Island, a ferry system. Alberta, Saskatchewan, and Manitoba did not obtain until 1930 the same control over Crown lands and natural resources which other provinces had. Newfoundland's long and detailed Terms of Union included a specific provision for the sale of oleomargarine. None of those differences altered the division of legislative powers between the provinces and the federal government.

Quebec in 1867 became an autonomous community only to the degree in which any state in a federation is autonomous. It could freely exercise its own autonomous provincial legislative powers in any way that did not conflict with the law of the Constitution. But in addition, the 1867 Constitution expanded Quebec's autonomy by guaranteeing that its citizens could participate in their own language in federal as well as provincial institutions of government. Writing in 1957, F.R. Scott observed:

> Quebec is and doubtless will remain a "homeland" to
> all French Canadians, except perhaps the Acadians,
> but this is an historic fact rather than a constitutional

rule. All Canada is the homeland for all Canadians. Canada is thus two cultures, but not two states, a federal system and not a dyarchy [government by two people or by two ruling authorities]. The ten provinces are equal in status and French culture, while geographically centred in Quebec, radiates outward through various social and political channels, but not through any special governmental institutions. The government of Quebec, although controlled by French Canadians, is neither French nor Catholic, being designed for all its inhabitants.

In any event, we will never know where the vision of Confederation's Fathers might have taken Canada. While the country was still in its adolescence, that vision was replaced by the phantasm of (to use the late Eugene Forsey's wonderful sobriquet) Confederation's wicked stepfathers.

CHAPTER 3

THE WICKED
STEPFATHERS

While the ship of state now sails on larger ventures and into foreign waters, she still retains the watertight compartments which are an essential part of her original structure.

— Lord Atkin, Judicial Committee of the
Privy Council, *ILO Conventions* case, 1937

THE ORIGINS OF THE JUDICIAL Committee of the Privy Council lie deep in the history of English constitutional development. It can be traced to the 1300s, when the Privy Council – comprising the private, personal advisers and favourites of the sovereign – took shape as the executive branch of government. In those days, the sovereign ruled as well as reigned and was, in addition, considered the source of justice to the people. The King's (or Queen's) privy councillors both administered government in the sovereign's name and advised the sovereign on petitions and appeals for justice. Thus was born the concept of a "judicial" Privy Council.

By the eighteenth century, the Privy Council's executive authority had been eclipsed by that of a cabinet responsible to Parliament. Its name, however, hung on, largely as symbolic nomenclature (by convention all cabinet ministers in both Britain and Canada are still designated as members of the Privy Council, and the senior civil service official in Canada has the title of Clerk of the Privy Council). The council's judicial role continued in more substantial form.

At first, the Privy Council's judicial committee was a loose and rather amorphous body. Its mandate was to review judgments of any court in the sovereign's dominions outside the United Kingdom, and none of the committee's members was required to have judicial experience. Technically, it was not a court at all, but a "board." It did not make "judgments"; rather it gave the sovereign "advice," and therefore its "advisements" required an executive order-in-council to give them legal effect. And because it "advised" the sovereign, it did not (until 1966) publish dissenting opinions, because by tradition the sovereign was not given conflicting advice.

By 1876, the Judicial Committee's membership had become largely restricted to Britain's most senior judges, the Lords of Appeal, known more familiarly as the "law lords." The law lords include the Lord Chancellor, the highest civil subject in the land (by tradition referred to as the "keeper of the King's conscience"), and all former lord chancellors.

Usually five members of the committee sat on a panel to hear a case. A critic wrote in 1894: "The personnel of that Court is as shifting as the Goodwin Sands. At one sitting it may be composed of the ablest judges in the land, and at the next sitting its chief characteristic may be senility. . . ." Half a century after their departure from the Canadian scene (in 1949), their influence on Canada's constitutional development is still debated with acrimony. Many legal and political science commentators view their contribution as almost unremittingly negative. Others are more moderate.

For example, University of British Columbia constitutional scholar Alan Cairns has written:

It is impossible to believe that a few elderly men in London deciding two or three constitutional cases a year precipitated, sustained and caused the development of Canada in a federalist direction the country would otherwise not have taken. It is evident that on occasion the provinces found an ally in the Privy Council, and that on balance they were aided in their struggles with the federal government. To attribute more than this to the Privy Council strains credulity. Courts are not self-starting institutions. They are called into play by groups and individuals seeking objectives that can be furthered by judicial support.

Cairns labels the Judicial Committee's critics left-wing centralists, anglophone nationalists, and "constitutional fundamentalists." He states that the JCPC's "great contribution – the injection of a decentralizing impulse into a constitutional structure too centralist for the diversity it had to contain and the placating of Quebec that was a consequence – was a positive influence in the evolution of Canadian federalism." He cites Pierre Trudeau: "[I]f the law lords had not leaned in the [provincial] direction, Quebec separation might not be a threat today; it might be an accomplished fact." Cairns reserves special condemnation for the centralist "fundamentalists" and their "perverse" appeal to the Fathers' intentions. He deprecates their intellectual rigour. He writes: "Their case is destroyed by its essential shallowness." Pursuit of the real meaning of the BNA Act, he says, is an exercise in futility, incapable of a

decisive outcome. Use of "ambiguous" pre-Confederation
material would not have improved the court's performance,
indeed might dangerously have allowed the horizon of 1867
"to restrict the measures of the future." "A living constitution," writes Cairns, "incorporates only so much of the past
as appears viable in the light of new conditions."

CLOTHING THE CONSTITUTION
There is an opposing view. No more fitting utterance can be
found to illustrate it than the one that leads this chapter.
Lord Atkin's "watertight compartments" tag sums up the
predominating view of Canada and its Constitution held
by the Judicial Committee of the Privy Council – a view in
large part totally at odds with the masonry of the Fathers of
Confederation. The law lords of the JCPC, for eighty-two
years the supreme legal arbiters of the Constitution, saw
watertight compartments where none was intended. They
saw the federal residual power (the POGG clause) as some
sort of fifth vehicular wheel, to be used only in times of
famine, pestilence, and war, otherwise giving way to a
more powerful provincial residual jurisdiction over property and civil rights. They saw the Dominion's power to
regulate trade and commerce as largely devoid of independent meaning. The Judicial Committee turned Canada's
Constitution inside out, shooed power out of Ottawa and
into the provinces, modelled the Canadian federation after
the American one – the exact antithesis of Macdonald's
nation-building – and even hamstrung the Canadian government's power to sign international treaties.

The law lords laboured under undoubted handicaps.
They were physically isolated from the country, and thus

largely ignorant of its political, economic, and social life. Their British experience lay outside of written constitutions altogether. There was a marked lack of consistency to both their judgments and the membership composition of their panels. They developed two absolutely opposing meanings of the POGG power. They disdained the use, in their interpretations, of either the *Confederation Debates* or the pre-Confederation resolutions from the Quebec City and London conferences. Their Lordships (particularly Lord Watson and Viscount Haldane) did not unconsciously or innocently distort the Constitution; they did it deliberately, boldly, and with premeditation. Here is Haldane's 1923 eulogy for Watson in the *Cambridge Law Journal*:

> Lord Watson put clothing upon the bones of the Constitution, and so covered them over with living flesh that the Constitution of Canada *took a new form* [emphasis ours]. The provinces were recognized as of equal authority co-ordinate with the Dominion, and a long series of decisions were given by him which solved many problems and produced a new contentment in Canada with the Constitution they had got in 1867. It is difficult to say what the extent of the debt was that Canada owed to Lord Watson. . . .

Difficult to say? Before the Canadian government succeeded – after seventy-five years of trying – in abolishing appeals to it, the Judicial Committee created what has been variously described as "legal chaos," a "legal morass," and a "constitutional mutilation." W.P.M. Kennedy, University of Toronto's founding dean of law and Canada's most influential constitutional analyst of the 1920s and 1930s, wrote:

"Seldom have statesmen [the Fathers of Confederation] more deliberately striven to write their purposes into law and seldom have these more signally failed before the judicial technique of statutory interpretation." McGregor Dawson dryly observed that the work of the JCPC "pointed the moral . . . on the futility of long-term political planning." Thanks to the law lords, in other words, the Fathers wasted a lot of time.

In any event, Viscount Haldane, who figured prominently in the JCPC's interpretations of the Canadian Constitution in the 1920s and 1930s, seemed certain that the Judicial Committee gave the Constitution "new form." So let's look at what it did.

POGG VERSUS PROPERTY AND CIVIL RIGHTS

In their reinterpretation of the BNA Act's division of federal and provincial powers, their Lordships advanced on two fronts.

Consumption of alcohol has been a seminal factor in Canadian federalism. In the early 1880s, the temperance movement in Canada was in full bloom. The movement, a powerful pan-Canadian force, was founded on the belief that self-discipline was essential to economic success and that alcohol was an obstacle to self-discipline. The temperance movement campaigned *nationally* for legal restrictions on alcohol's manufacture and sale. Jurisdiction over the trade in Canada was shared by the two levels of government. The provinces could prohibit retail sale, whereas the federal government could prohibit the manufacture of alcohol and regulate wholesale and interprovincial trade. Neither level of government was enthusiastic about prohibition, since it would cause losses of tax revenue and partisan support. Their solution was a compromise known as "local option" (embodied in the federal Canada Temperance Act of 1878) which gave local governments (creatures of the provinces) the right to prohibit the retail sale of alcohol. Which introduces Charles Russell, a Fredericton tavern owner.

Russell was convicted under the 1878 act of illegally selling liquor. His lawyer appealed to the Judicial Committee to decide if the Dominion government had acted *ultra vires* (beyond its constitutional powers) in passing the Canada Temperance Act, legislation which clearly encroached on provincial jurisdiction over licences, property and civil rights, and "local matters." Their Lordships, in *Russell v. The Queen* (1882), said no. They said that, to secure public order – that is, peace, order and good government (POGG) – throughout the country in the implementation of a temperance scheme, Parliament could prohibit the sale of liquor even though there might be some "incidental interference" with provincial jurisdiction. Sir Montague Smith, writing for the JCPC, said:

What Parliament is dealing with in legislation of this kind is not a matter in relation to property and its rights, but one relating to public order and safety. . . . Few, if any, laws could be made by Parliament for the peace, order and good government of Canada which did not in some incidental way affect property and civil rights, and it could not have been intended, when assuring to the provinces exclusive legislative authority on the subjects of property and civil rights, to exclude the Parliament from the exercise of this general power [POGG] whenever any such incidental interference would result from it.

In other words, the decisive factor in determining jurisdiction was the primary purpose of the law, and its scope. If the issue was of nationwide importance, the Dominion could take jurisdiction under the POGG power. Sir John A. could not have put it better.

Four years later, however, *Russell* was dismembered by Lord Watson, the clothier of the Constitution. In the *Local Prohibition* case (1896), he declared that the enumerated federal powers in Section 91, rather than being illustrations ("for greater certainty," to quote the BNA Act) of POGG, were a self-standing and inclusive list, analogous to the precise provincial powers enumerated in Section 92. He then made what McGregor Dawson has called "the astounding discovery" that the POGG power, now severed from its Section 91 illustrations, was not the Dominion's general power, or the paramount essence of Dominion authority, but a supplement to its enumerated powers. Lord Watson wrote:

The exercise of legislative power by the Parliament of Canada, in regard to all matters not enumerated in Section 91, ought to be strictly confined to such matters as are unquestionably of Canadian interest and importance, and ought not to trench upon provincial legislation with respect to any of the classes of subjects enumerated in Section 92. To attach *any other construction* to the general power [POGG], which, *in supplement of its enumerated powers*, is confirmed upon the Parliament of Canada by Section 91, would, in their

Lordships' opinion, not only be contrary to the intend-
ment of the Act, but would practically destroy the
autonomy of the provinces [emphasis ours].

The Judicial Committee realized, of course, that some
sort of meaning had to be invested in POGG. Thus, over the
next few years, it created the "emergency doctrine," immor-
tally articulated by Viscount Haldane in *Toronto Electric
Commissioners v. Snider* (1925):

> Their Lordships think that the decision in *Russell v.
> The Queen* can only be supported today . . . on the
> assumption of the Board [the JCPC], apparently made
> at the time of deciding the case of *Russell v. The Queen*,
> that the evil of intemperance at that time amounted
> in Canada to one so great and so general and pressing
> that the National Parliament was called on to inter-
> vene to protect the nation from disaster. An epidemic
> of pestilence might conceivably have been regarded as
> analogous.

At other points, the Judicial Committee added famine
and war to pestilence and, having emasculated POGG – no
pestilence, famine, or war, no POGG – turned to expanding
provincial powers.

The only language in the Constitution as vague and
general as "peace, order and good government" is the provincial jurisdiction over "property and civil rights." The latter
phrase, like the former, was not new constitutional language in Canada in 1867. Reference to property and civil
rights appeared in the Quebec Act, 1774, which restored
French civil law as the private law of the conquered colony,

as opposed to the "public law" of British colonial administration. It appeared again in 1792 in the first act of the
legislature of the newly created province of Upper Canada
– this time signifying that Upper Canada (Ontario), as distinct from Lower Canada (Quebec), was adopting English
common law. It can be surmised that, by 1867, the authors
of the BNA Act understood "property and civil rights" to
mean what Osgoode Hall's Peter Hogg calls "a compendious
description of the entire body of private law which governs
the relationships between subject and subject, as opposed to
the law which governs the relationships between the subject
and the institutions of government." In sum, it cut a very
wide swath, so wide that, if the BNA Act's authors had not
moved to limit the definition of property and civil rights,
there would have been very little left for the Dominion
Parliament to do.

With few minor exceptions, the JCPC proceeded to rule
from the nineteenth century into the twentieth that provincial legislatures could claim exclusive jurisdiction over government interventions into the marketplace – whether it be
to regulate commerce, establish standards for employment,
or settle labour disputes. Thus, while the Fathers thought
they had created a federal state in which the central government would retain general power over everything not
specifically delegated to the provinces, the exact opposite
developed: the provinces were increasingly granted power
to legislate on anything not specifically assigned to the
Dominion government. In effect, the residual power slipped
away from the Dominion, to be replaced by "property and
civil rights" as the residual clause.

The 1867 Constitution had assigned to the provinces
responsibility for education, roads, social welfare, relief for

the poor, hospitals, some pensions, and matters of a similar "local" nature, all enumerated in the sixteen subclauses of Section 92 of the BNA Act. Until the last years of the nineteenth century, these had created little federal–provincial conflict. The Dominion showed little interest in getting into any of these areas, and the provinces, as a result, had not had to fight for their jurisdiction. The Privy Council's interpretations of the Constitution led, in the words of the report of the Royal Commission on Dominion–Provincial Relations (1937), the Rowell–Sirois Commission, "to a competition between the specific enumerated heads of Section 91 and 92. In this competition, the provinces enjoyed an advantage because Section 92 contained two heads capable of a general and inclusive signification, namely, 'property and civil rights in the province' and 'generally all matters of a merely local or private nature in the province' while Section 91 contained only one such [specifically enumerated] head, 'the regulation of trade and commerce' and it received a restricted interpretation [from the JCPC]."

TRADE AND COMMERCE POWER

The JCPC was not content with diminishing the POGG power; it took the same approach to the "trade and commerce" power, with the result that the provincial power over "property and civil rights" assumed astonishing new dimensions. When the Fathers of Confederation assigned jurisdiction over the "regulation of trade and commerce" to Parliament, they intended that the national government play an important role in the economic life of the new nation – for the benefit of all its citizens – while preventing pre-Confederation's nineteenth-century parochial provincial economic policies and barriers to trade. The Canadian federal power was meant to be broader than the equivalent clause in the American Constitution, which restricted the federal government to regulating "commerce with foreign nations and among the several States, and with the Indian tribes" and yet it has turned out to be much more limited.

What the Privy Council declared was that a provincial law in relation to property and civil rights did not conflict with the Dominion's trade and commerce power, because all that the federal power meant was "*political arrangements in regard to trade requiring the sanction of Parliament, regulation of trade in matters of inter-provincial concern, and it may be* that they [Dominion powers] would include general regulation of trade affecting the whole Dominion [emphasis ours]."

The defining Judicial Committee decision was the *Board of Commerce* case (1922), dealing with federal legislation that regulated profiteering, hoarding, and charging excessive prices for "the necessities of life," matters which might be reasonably assumed to be in the interest of the nation. Viscount Haldane wrote, in what Hogg in *The Constitutional Law of Canada* calls "one uninformative sentence," that the federal trade and commerce power had no meaning independent of other provisions in the Constitution. Thus there might be economic forces in the country which ignored provincial boundaries but they were "not sufficient to carry them out of property and civil rights and into the federal fold."

This narrow interpretation of the trade and commerce power – rather than providing Canadians with, in Haldane's words, "a new contentment" with their Constitution – produced jurisdictional chaos and conflict. The federal government was compelled to try to develop a Canadian common market by means of criminal law, credit control, and international trade agreements rather than through the obvious and natural mechanism of the clearly defined trade and commerce power.

To exert its authority in an area as nationally important as the wheat trade, it had to resort to declaring Prairie grain elevators to be "works for the general advantage of Canada." The Dominion government's "exclusive" power to regulate fisheries became no longer "exclusive." Once a fish was packed and processed, the Judicial Committee ruled it was subject to provincial control. Likewise, once a potato was packed for sale, it no longer could fall within the concurrent federal legislative power over agriculture. According to the JCPC, marketing of agricultural products fell within a provincial Natural Products Marketing Act and was ruled to be a matter of "property and civil rights." A federal Marketing Act of similar scope was ruled invalid because it encroached on provincial jurisdiction.

Viscount Haldane and his colleagues delivered the *coup de grâce* when the JCPC overruled the Supreme Court of Canada and held that a provincial company could do business outside provincial boundaries if granted permission by the outside authority – that is, by another province. Thus, nationwide trade and commerce could be carried out and regulated by provincial bodies. This was the ultimate diminution of the federal influence: the national government was irrelevant, interprovincial co-operation was sufficient. There was no need for Ottawa to speak for Canada – the provinces jointly could do it, however incoherent and ineffective they might be. W.P.M. Kennedy, summarizing the court's cumulative effect, said the trade and commerce

power had been "relegated to a position utterly impossible
to defend on the clearest terms of the [BNA] Act, and one
which makes any reliance on it barren and useless."

NEW DEAL, BAD DEAL

In 1932, the Judicial Committee said the Dominion had
jurisdiction over aeronautics (permitting the creation of
Trans-Canada Airlines, predecessor to Air Canada, as a
federal Crown corporation). This wasn't so much an inconsistency with the court's provincialist tilt as it was a decision
based primarily on a British Empire treaty that was binding
to Canada.* In the same year, via the same treaty route, the
Judicial Committee also gave the Dominion jurisdiction
over radio broadcasting (permitting the establishment of
the Canadian Broadcasting Corporation), although in this
case it unexpectedly revived POGG – stating that, because
the Fathers of Confederation had not conceived of Canada
signing treaties in her own name, this "gap" (not surprisingly, this is known as the constitutional "gap" doctrine)

---

* Section 132 of the BNA Act gave the Dominion Parliament "all powers
necessary for performing the obligations of Canada or of any province
thereof arising under any treaty between the Empire and foreign countries," the principle being that the Empire spoke with one voice because,
prior to 1931, only the Empire – which really meant the Imperial government of Great Britain – had an international legal personality. This decision was rendered after Canada severed its last colonial ties with Britain
under the 1931 Statute of Westminster, but it still applied until the treaty
was renounced in 1947 and replaced by another treaty to which Canada
was a party in its own name. Given the Judicial Committee's decision in
the 1937 *Labour Conventions* case (see below), the Dominion government arguably was no longer entitled to aeronautics jurisdiction.

could be covered by the POGG power. This was not a conversion, merely a hiccup. Five years later, the Judicial Committee reverted to its previous view.

In 1935, at the depth of the Great Depression – with thousands upon thousands of Canadians poor and unemployed – the Dominion government of Prime Minister R.B. Bennett introduced an ambitious and long overdue "New Deal" program (named after similar social-welfare reform legislation in the United States) that provided for unemployment insurance, maximum working hours, minimum wages, and a weekly day of rest (much of this emanating from draft conventions of the International Labour Organization in Geneva); control over price-spreads to combat profiteering and predatory price-cutting; legislation enabling the creation of a national agricultural products marketing system; and a mechanism to enable debt-ridden farmers to retain mortgaged farms by renegotiating their debts. The Judicial Committee in 1937 ruled most of the New Deal program invalid, declaring that, for the most part, it constituted a federal intrusion into provincial jurisdiction which the economic trauma of the Depression was not sufficient to warrant. War, pestilence, and famine – real famine – it had to be before the Dominion government could act.

The unemployment insurance and agricultural marketing schemes were said by the JCPC to invade the domain of private contract (under "property and civil rights"), even though, in the case of marketing legislation, it was universally desired throughout the country, and all nine provinces (Newfoundland did not join Canada until 1949) had enacted complementary legislation at federal request. As for the unemployment insurance legislation, wrote Lord Atkin, "it is sufficient to say that the present Act does not purport to

deal with any special emergency. It founds itself in the preamble on general world-wide conditions. . . ."

Most notoriously, the Judicial Committee concluded
that, while the Parliament of Canada as a colony possessed
full legislative authority to assume obligations under international treaties, the Parliament of Canada as a sovereign
nation did not. The committee's reasoning was as follows.

The International Labour Organization had adopted a
series of conventions under which a number of its member
states – Canada was one – agreed to enact laws that limited
employee working hours and created a minimum wage and
a day of weekly rest. The federal government ratified the
conventions in 1935, and introduced appropriate legislation
into Parliament. The JCPC said the legislation was invalid
because the power to regulate hours of work and wages fell
under property and civil rights. Lord Atkin, who wrote their
Lordships' opinion, also said that what Canada (that is, the
Dominion Parliament) could do by means of Section 132 of
the BNA Act "as part of the British Empire," she could not
do "by virtue of her new status as an international person."
He wrote: "While it is true . . . that it was not contemplated
in 1867 that the Dominion would possess treaty-making
powers, it is impossible to strain the section [132 of the BNA
Act] so as to cover the uncontemplated event" – although
the JCPC had done precisely that, strained the section, five
years earlier in awarding the federal Parliament jurisdiction over radio broadcasting. However, in Lord Atkins's reasoning, in classifying (under either Section 91 or Section 92)
a statute which was required to implement a Canadian
treaty, one had to disregard that its purpose was to implement a treaty. If the statute related to a matter allocated
under Section 91, the federal Parliament had the power to

implement it. If, on the other hand, the statute related to a matter under Section 92, the provinces had to implement it.

Two other decisions by the Judicial Committee merit special note. Opinions written by Lord Watson in 1892 and Viscount Haldane in 1916[*] had the effect of conferring on provincial lieutenant-governors the same status in relation to provincial legislatures as possessed by the governor general vis-à-vis the federal Parliament. In other words, their Lordships gave Canada multiple but co-equal Crowns, the watertight-compartment framework of sovereign provinces side by side with a sovereign Dominion – which, fundamentally, is the shape of contemporary Canadian federalism.

ABOLITION OF JUDICIAL COMMITTEE APPEALS

Beginning in 1875, when the Dominion Parliament created the Supreme Court of Canada, the federal government with varying degrees of enthusiasm sought to terminate the Judicial Committee's jurisdiction over Canadian affairs. It got part way in 1888, amending the Criminal Code to end the Judicial Committee's authority to hear criminal appeals. But getting rid of it entirely was more difficult, both legally and politically. The legal barriers were the most insurmountable. The JCPC's jurisdiction in Canada was supported not only by Imperial statutory authority, but also by the royal prerogative – a vague but significant power embedded in the common law. On the one hand, the Dominion and provincial legislatures were prohibited from enacting laws deemed "repugnant" to (in conflict with)

---

[*] Respectively, *Liquidators of the Maritime Bank v. Receiver-General of New Brunswick* and *Bonanza Creek Gold Mining Co. Ltd. v. The King*

Imperial statutes (which is what British statutes were called when they specifically applied to the colonies). On the other hand, it was thought that a colonial legislature – however self-governing the colony might be – did not possess the authority to intrude by statute onto the royal prerogative, in this case the right of a subject to carry his or her appeal to the foot of the Throne. When, thirty-eight years after it was passed, the 1888 amendment to the Criminal Code got to the Judicial Committee, their Lordships were waiting. In *Nadan v. The King*, they declared that the Dominion Parliament had acted *ultra vires* in ending criminal appeals to the Judicial Committee because the Criminal Code amendment was both in conflict with two Imperial statutes and an extraterritorial application of Canadian law. The decision had the effect of further convincing the federal government that the time had come to step out of the Imperial embrace. It pressed for an Imperial conference that year, 1926, out of which came a declaration stating that the United Kingdom and the self-governing Dominions (including Australia, New Zealand, Newfoundland, South Africa, and the Irish Free State as well as Canada)

> are autonomous communities within the British Empire, equal in status, in no way subordinate to one to another in any aspect of their domestic or external affairs, although united by a common allegiance to the Crown, and freely associated as the British Commonwealth of Nations.

The declaration resulted, five years later, in the United Kingdom enacting the Statute of Westminster, which

conferred on the Dominions the power to repeal or amend
Imperial statutes which applied to them. Shortly thereafter,
Canada re-enacted the 1888 Criminal Code amendment,
which was held by the courts to be valid. The federal government, however, did not embark on the final steps to
remove the Judicial Committee's jurisdiction until the flood
of national dismay over the JCPC's handling of the New
Deal legislation. In 1939, the federal government introduced
a bill in Parliament to abolish remaining Judicial Committee
appeals. It also referred the bill to the Supreme Court of
Canada to test its validity. Clearly Section 101 of the BNA Act
authorized the abolition of appeals to the JCPC from the
Supreme Court of Canada. But there was the lingering issue
of *per saltum* ("by leaps and bounds") appeals directly from
provincial courts to the Judicial Committee, bypassing the
Supreme Court of Canada. The Supreme Court was asked
to determine if *per saltum* appeals fell under the Section 92
head of "the administration of justice in the province."
The Supreme Court said the bill fell within federal competence and, as of December 23, 1949, no case commencing in
the courts could be appealed beyond the Supreme Court
of Canada. Cases that had commenced before that date,
however, could still be heard by the elderly men in London,
who performed their last Canadian act in 1959. They ended
their interpretation of Canada's Constitution more or less
as they began it, with inconsistency. To the last, they swung
between two competing interpretations of POGG, with
Lord Simon abandoning the "emergency doctrine" in 1946[*]

---

[*] *Attorney-General of Ontario v. Canada Temperance Federation.* Alcohol
again.

only to have Lord Wright bring it back the following year.[*]
After appeals to the JCPC ended, the Supreme Court of
Canada crept back toward the Simon position, but not all
the way. Watson, Haldane, et al., have never been undone.

WATSON, HALDANE et al.: FOOTSTEPS IN CONCRETE
One may find general agreement on these lasting impacts of
the JCPC's rulings (the list is not complete, and it does not
purport to be anything approaching a scholarly political,
social, and economic analysis):

 • The Judicial Committee's decisions ended the quasi-
 Imperial relationship Ottawa had with the provinces in
 its constitutional role as post-1867 successor to the
 Imperial government. McGregor Dawson, no fan of their
 Lordships, allows that their enlargement of provincial
 rights in the decades before and after the turn of the
 century was not as shocking as many would like to believe,
 "and it was, in fact, in substantial accord with the
 general trend of opinion in Canada."
 • The law lords' role as the final judicial authority in all
 civil cases, and the ready availability of *per saltum* appeals
 (it has been estimated that about half the cases the JCPC
 heard came via this route) meant the Supreme Court of
 Canada was denied an important role in developing law
 in the country.
 • The law lords' ruling on the federal government's treaty
 power caused (in W.H. McConnell's understatement)

---

[*] *Cooperative Committee on Japanese Canadians v. Attorney-General of
Canada*

"considerable Canadian diplomatic inconvenience" – or, in the more forceful opinion of other critics, a contractual incapacity shared by few other federal states. A major constitutional limitation on Canada's international relations was imposed on the nation in the very decade when she finally achieved full independence. Since that ruling, the Canadian government has felt required to include a so-called federal clause in treaties and conventions, where the subject matter either falls under provincial jurisdiction or is divided between the two levels of government. The "federal clause" permits provinces to sign on individually to implement provisions affecting provincial matters.

• Their lordships' evisceration of the POGG power thwarted the more cohesive development of the country at the very time when governments of the industrialized democracies were beginning to intervene in the marketplace to build the welfare state. By determining, in effect, that it would be the provinces, not the Dominion, which would be the prime "interveners" (under the property and civil rights power), the JCPC thrust on them what former Chief Justice Bora Laskin called a "destructive negative autonomy." They were unequally able – where they were able at all – to meet the economic and social problems of a rapidly urbanizing, rapidly growing twentieth-century society. The country was close to chaos, and several provinces close to collapse, when the Bennett government introduced its New Deal legislation. The law lords who boasted that they put clothes on the Constitution did not see the country that the Constitution governed.

CHAPTER 4

HOME ALONE (ALMOST)

*We are making for a harbour which was not the harbour
I foresaw twenty-five years ago, but it is a good harbour.*
— Wilfrid Laurier, 1911

OUR CONSTITUTIONAL JOURNEY now follows Canada
from colonial adolescent to sovereign adult, from restless-
ness under imperialism into a new labyrinth of federal–
provincial constitutional engagements around the building
of the welfare state and, finally, to the very edge, the very lip,
of full mastery over our own Constitution. It is a period
lasting seven decades.

At the turn of the century Sir Wilfrid Laurier, prime
minister since 1896, put in words the Good Destiny Myth
with his declaration that, as the nineteenth century had
belonged to the United States, the twentieth century would
belong to Canada. The Good Destiny Myth, welcome as it
was to the majority of Laurier's fellow citizens, nonetheless
masked huge potholes. To cite one difficulty, the reality of
Confederation's promise of a national economy was that
Ontario and Quebec, the most heavily populated areas,
received the great majority of new investment. To cite
another, the massive increase in Canada's population – from
5.4 million in 1901 to almost 9 million in 1921, largely the
result of immigration, had serious implications, particularly

for French-speaking groups outside Quebec, and the linguistic balance of the entire country.

Enter Henri Bourassa, grandson of 1837 rebel Louis-Joseph Papineau, and a French-Canadian nationalist of a very different stripe from the separatists of the late twentieth century. He was to become a major contributor to full Canadian independence.

He was elected as a follower of Laurier's in 1896, but split with the Liberal leader in 1899 over Laurier's decision to send troops into the South African War between Britain and the Afrikaaner republics. Most French Canadians viewed militant British imperialism as a threat to their survival and sympathized with the Afrikaaners. Most English Canadians, on the other hand, supported the British cause. Laurier, under intense Anglo-Canadian pressure, reluctantly authorized recruitment of a token one thousand infantrymen. Articulate, astute, courageous, and brilliant, Bourassa kindled a vigorous movement in French-speaking Canada – and, indeed, for a time, throughout the country – around three major themes: Canada's relationship with Britain; the relationship of French culture to English culture; and the values that should guide economic life. He launched a mission to warn all Canadians, but especially French Canadians, of the dangers of imperialism. He strongly promoted the view that Canada's Parliament alone – not the Imperial Parliament in London – had the authority to declare Canada to be at war. He became the spokesperson for French-language minorities across Canada, promoting his belief in a bicultural, autonomous Canada that would be home to French Canadians from sea to sea. He warned that cultural duality was an absolute condition for French Canadians to continue to accept Confederation. He

campaigned, unsuccessfully, in 1905, for the rights of francophones in the new provinces of Alberta and Saskatchewan.

Laurier, for his part, found it impossible to achieve
a national consensus on Canada's place in the Empire, a
dilemma which equally plagued his successor, Sir Robert
Borden. In 1917, at the height of the slaughter of the First
World War, Borden returned from a visit to the trenches,
determined to impose compulsory military service on
Canadians. He offered a political coalition in a Union
Government to Laurier, then leader of the opposition, to
further the war effort. Laurier refused, stating that Quebec
would never accept conscription and that, if he joined a
pro-conscription coalition government, Quebec would be
delivered politically into the hands of Bourassa's nationalists. In the election of 1917, the country divided on linguistic lines, and the Conservatives, though re-elected, were left
with a heavy liability in Quebec.

The conscription crisis served as midwife to the birth
of a minor secessionist movement in Quebec led by priest-
historian Abbé Lionel Groulx. Groulx – opposed by
Bourassa, his one-time mentor, who remained wedded to
pan-Canadianism – developed, by means of a revisionist
historical examination of Quebec's post-Conquest period,
a view of the Conquest as French Canada's disaster.[*] He
had difficulty convincing many Quebeckers beyond the
Montreal clerical and intellectual community that their
future was in jeopardy, however, especially when Quebec
politicians such as Ernest Lapointe wielded so much influence in the governing Liberal party in Ottawa. By 1927,

---

[*] He also promoted the idea of a new Quebec state, to be called
Laurentia.

Groulx admitted that, though Canada was an "anemic giant" infected with "many germs of dissolution," it might still be revived and reformed.

In Groulx, there was the foreshadowing of contemporary Quebec separatists. After Groulx's death in 1967 – Canada's centennial year – there is, perhaps, irony in the fact that Claude Ryan, editor of *Le Devoir*, the newspaper which Bourassa founded, commemorated Groulx as the spiritual father of modern Quebec. The most immediate manifestation of Bourassa's legacy (he died in 1952) was that Mackenzie King, who succeeded Laurier as Liberal leader in 1919, endorsed the view that only Canada's Parliament could send Canada into war. Indeed, it was King, as prime minister, who fulfilled Sir John A. Macdonald's dream of a nation co-equal with Britain. An outline of the rather tortuous path to independence follows:

- *1871.* Under the Treaty of Washington, a joint high commission is established to settle outstanding issues between Britain and the United States. Sir John A. Macdonald, as Canada's prime minister, is made a member of the British delegation to represent Canadian interests. He feels outnumbered. The widespread feeling in Canada is that Britain sacrifices Canadian interests to achieve harmony with the United States.
- *1879.* A Canadian high commission is established in London to provide direct contact between the Imperial and Canadian governments, end-running the formal constitutional conduit of the governor general.
- *1887.* The first Colonial Conference is held. Britain proposes the creation of an Imperial council to discuss governmental issues with its colonies. Canada accepts

the idea only if it does not entail a reduction of autonomy.

• *1899*. The South African Boer War begins. Although Canada is automatically at war as part of the British Empire, the Canadian government insists on determining the extent of Canada's participation. Prime Minister Wilfrid Laurier ultimately sends only volunteers and stresses that the Canadian involvement is not to be regarded as a precedent.

• *1897*. A British–U.S. joint high commission is established to settle Canadian–American disputes, most notably the location of the Alaskan panhandle boundary. This time, Canadians are appointed as two of the three British commissioners. However, the British appointee supports his three American counterparts against the Canadians. This strengthens Canada's resolve to conduct her own foreign affairs.

• *1909*. The Canadian government creates its own Department of External Affairs. In the same year, the International Joint Commission is established to regulate the use of boundary waters – the first permanent Canada–United States organization. All Canadian commissioners are Canadian but formally appointed by the British government.

• *1914*. Britain declares war against Germany on behalf of the entire Empire. Again, Canada decides the extent of its participation (which is considerable). Canadian troops enter the First World War under British command, but by 1917 they form a Canadian corps under General Currie.

• *1917*. Britain convenes the first meeting of the Imperial War Cabinet, consisting of the prime ministers of Britain and various Dominions and India.

- *1918.* Britain acquiesces to demands that the Dominions participate in their own right at the peace conference.
- *1919.* Canada and the other Dominions sign the Treaty of Versailles in their own right, although as members of the Empire and not independent countries. (Canada later becomes a member of the League of Nations, forerunner to the United Nations, and in 1927 is elected to a term on the League's Council.)
- *1922.* The Chanak crisis. Without prior consultation with the Empire, Britain informs Turkey that war with Britain means war with the Empire. Canada's prime minister, Mackenzie King, informs Britain that only the Parliament of Canada will decide whether Canada goes to war.
- *1923.* At Canada's insistence, the British government designates the Canadian Minister of Marine and Fisheries to sign a Halibut Treaty with the United States.
- *1926.* The Imperial Conference agrees that the Dominions should have effective independence. The report of the conference, known as the Balfour Declaration, describes Canada and the other Dominions as "autonomous communities within the British empire, equal in status, in no way subordinate to one another in any aspect of their domestic or external affairs, though united by a common allegiance to the Crown, and freely associated as members of the British Commonwealth [later called just the Commonwealth]."

The Balfour Declaration further states that the governor general of each Dominion is "the representative of the Crown, holding in all essential respects the same position in relation to the administration of public affairs in the dominion as is held by His Majesty the King in Great Britain." The Imperial government relinquishes its power to reserve or disallow Canadian legislation, and repeals the Colonial Laws Validity Act.

• *1927.* Canada appoints its first diplomatic representative to a non-Empire country – the United States. The United States reciprocates.

• *1928.* Britain appoints its first high commissioner to Canada, now that the governor general represents only the monarch, not the Imperial (British) government.

• *1931.* Britain's Parliament enacts the Statute of Westminster, confirming the Balfour Declaration and Canada's independence. No Canadian law will henceforth be declared void because of a conflict with British law, and no British law will apply to Canada except with Canada's consent. In addition, Canada acquires the right of extra-territoriality – the right to legislate for its citizens outside the state. However, there is no Canadian political agreement on how to amend Canada's constitution, the BNA Act, which is a British statute. Thus the formal amending mechanism is left with the British Parliament at Westminster.

Premiers Howard Ferguson of Ontario and Louis-Alexandre Taschereau of Quebec decided in 1927 that the Imperial legal draftsmen were probably heading down a road that would lead to the Canadian federal Parliament receiving from Westminster the power to amend any part of the BNA Act by simple federal statute. They therefore demanded that the colonial practice remain unchanged – whereby the Constitution could be amended by the British Parliament only upon receipt of a "joint address" by Canada's two Houses of Parliament. The result was that Canada's full independence remained bridled by an important technical hitch.

• *1947.* The Letters Patent declare that the governor general shall legally exercise virtually all the sovereign's constitutional powers in relation to Canada. (Although, interestingly enough, not for another thirty years are those full powers exercised, by Governor General Jules Léger.) In the same year, Parliament enacts Canada's first Citizenship Act, declaring, for the first time, Canadians to be citizens of their own country (the act, in addition, declares that they are also British subjects).

• *1949.* The Supreme Court of Canada is declared Canada's highest court of appeal, replacing Britain's Judicial Committee of the Privy Council.

• *1982.* Proclamation by the Queen of the Constitution Act, 1982, at last gives Canada a mechanism to amend its own Constitution, thus terminating the last legal vestige of British colonial control.

NEW HARBOUR, MANY WAVES

The remainder of this chapter deals with the social, economic, and political issues that form the backdrop to Canadian constitutional developments over the first seven decades of the twentieth century. It was a busy time for a national government required to respond to many new national priorities and shape new approaches to economic and social policy making.

In the period immediately following the First World War, the Dominion government was confronted by two regional revolts. The first was by Western farmers who wanted a new National Policy based on free trade, nation-alization of railways, and direct democracy. They united with dissident Liberals to form the Progressive movement, which elected sixty-five members to Parliament in 1921 and permanently broke the two-party tradition of federal poli-tics. The second revolt was spearheaded by the Maritime Rights movement and was fuelled by discontent with the region's declining influence in Confederation and its inabil-ity to protect such regional interests as protective tariffs, federal subsidies, transportation, and port development. The Progressive movement disintegrated through lack of cohesion and the return of agricultural prosperity. The Maritime Rights movement was undermined by Prime Minister King's appointment of a commission of inquiry into Maritimes discontent (which resolved little but, in ster-ling Canadian political tradition, bought time).

A fledgling women's movement had emerged during the war, and in 1917 women were given the vote (except in Quebec, where they had to wait until 1941). In 1929, the courts ruled that women were legal "persons," thus allowing them to be appointed to the Senate. The final decision, it should be noted, was delivered by the Judicial Committee of the Privy Council, which called the exclusion of women from public office "a relic of days more barbarous than ours."

THE DEPRESSION:
JCPC CHICKENS COME HOME TO ROOST
As historians have recorded, few countries were affected as severely as Canada by the Great Depression of the 1930s – a severity aggravated by the Depression's uneven impact, the country's rudimentary social-welfare structure, and

misguided government policies. Between 1929 and 1933, gross national expenditure declined by 42 per cent. By 1933, 30 per cent of the labour force was unemployed, and one in five Canadians was dependent upon government relief. Because a third of gross national income was derived from exports, Canada was particularly affected by the collapse in world trade. The four Western provinces, which depended almost exclusively on primary-product exports, felt the greatest impact. In Saskatchewan, which was plagued by crop failures and the lowest price for wheat in history, total provincial income plummeted by 90 per cent within two years, forcing two-thirds of the rural population onto relief. The other Western provinces were technically bankrupt from 1932 onwards. Although Ontario and Québec experienced heavy unemployment, they were less severely afflicted because of their more diversified industrial economies, which produced for the protected domestic market. The Maritimes had entered into severe economic decline in the 1920s and had less distance to fall. The burden of the Depression was also unequally distributed between classes. Although wages dropped throughout the 1930s, prices declined even faster. As a result, the standard of living of property owners and those with jobs increased. Farmers, young people, small-business owners, and the unemployed bore the brunt of economic hardship.

The unrest in the country which the Depression caused found expression in new political movements.

The socialist Co-operative Commonwealth Federation emerged in 1932 as a coalition of farmers, labour leaders, and intellectuals (and remnants of the old Progressive movement). Its Regina Manifesto of 1933 called for national unemployment insurance and health insurance, public housing, agricultural price supports, and laws to protect farmers against their creditors.

In 1935, the Social Credit movement took shape in Alberta, led by evangelist William "Bible Bill" Aberhart, who became premier in 1935. Social Credit's adherents – who seemed not to exist in large numbers outside Alberta – believed economic hardship was the product of an inefficient capitalist system which failed to put enough money into the hands of people to enjoy the fruits of their labours. This could be rectified by the government issuing money to consumers – "social credit" – to purchase goods and services produced; thus the Social Credit party sought to disconnect the province from Ottawa's monetary control. The doctrine proved, among other things, constitutionally impossible because fiscal and monetary policy was outside provincial jurisdiction. The party disconnected itself from Social Credit fundamentalism, and governed Alberta as a small-c conservative party until 1971. (The Social Credit Party also governed British Columbia for about thirty years, but never paid attention to the doctrine.)

A new nationalist political party, the Union Nationale, emerged in Quebec under Maurice Duplessis. He became premier in 1936 with the aim of strengthening Quebec vis-à-vis Ottawa and eventually achieving Quebec autonomy.

THE PROVINCIAL BARONS SAY NO
Nationally, the Depression resulted in the Liberal government of Mackenzie King appointing a Royal Commission on Dominion–Provincial Relations (the Rowell–Sirois Commission) to examine the distribution of constitutional powers and the financial arrangements of the federal system.

By then it was clear that the new social responsibilities –
essentially placed on provincial shoulders (in no small part
by decisions of the Judicial Committee of the Privy Council)
– could not be financed adequately since Ottawa retained
the largest sources of revenue. Indeed, the Depression had
forced Ottawa to underwrite provincial outlays for relief
and provincial debt service as well as to provide extra-
constitutional subsidies.

The commission recommended that the federal government take responsibility for unemployment insurance and
the establishment of a system of national adjustment grants
for the provinces – the forerunner of equalization payments
to poorer provinces. Although King obtained the consent of
the provinces for a constitutional amendment allowing
Ottawa to enact unemployment insurance legislation, the
premiers of Alberta, Ontario, and Quebec – the three
wealthiest provinces – rejected the other recommendations
and railed against what they labelled the commission's centralist thrust.

Despite these provincialist obstacles, however, King's
administration set off down the path of more activist government. The constitutional amendment of 1940 permitted unemployment insurance to be added to the 1927 Old Age
Pension. The latter was a curious hybrid: created by federal
statute, jointly financed by federal and provincial governments, and administered by the provinces because pensions
were considered a provincial constitutional responsibility.
The OAP paid $20 a month, depending on other income and
assets, and was available to British subjects seventy years of
age or older, with at least twenty years' residency in Canada.
Eligibility was subject to a strict means test widely regarded
as humiliating.

In 1944, the federal family allowance was introduced, giving mothers a monthly cheque for child care. This was Canada's first universal welfare program, paid without reference to recipients' income or assets. It was recommended in the 1943 national plan for postwar reconstruction (*Report on Social Security for Canada* – the Marsh Report), a comprehensive attack on poverty and economic insecurity based upon a broad scheme of social insurance supported by universal family allowances, a national health system, and a large-scale national employment program. King selected one element of the proposed plan – family allowances – as a vote-getting device in the next federal election. This manoeuvre permitted him to outflank the Left in Canadian politics, which was making electoral gains. (In 1943, the CCF formed the official opposition in Ontario and, in 1944, formed North America's first socialist government in Saskatchewan.) From a constitutional viewpoint, family allowances were seen as falling comfortably within the federal government's spending power; thus, few provincial hackles were raised.

During the Second World War, Canada operated essentially as a unitary state. The impact on the Canadian tax structure was profound. To equitably distribute the enormous financial burden of the war, to raise funds efficiently, and to minimize the impact of inflation, the major tax sources were gathered under a central fiscal authority. Under the War-Time Tax Agreements, 1941–45, the provinces agreed to surrender the personal and corporate income tax fields to the federal government for the duration of the war and for one year thereafter; in exchange they received fixed annual payments.

The Dominion bureaucracy grew from 46,000 in 1939 to 116,000 in 1945. The federal government functioned under its emergency powers – technically, the 1914 War Measures Act. No fewer than 6,414 orders were issued under the legislation, which allowed the government to act without recourse to Parliament. Federal emergency regulations extended to transportation (air, rail, and road), petroleum products, hydro-electricity, construction materials, supplies for the war effort, scarce commodities for civilian life, and so on. By war's end, 85 per cent of the non-agricultural workforce fell under federal jurisdiction.

On August 6, 1945, on the day the atomic bomb was dropped on Hiroshima, Prime Minister King opened the Dominion–Provincial Conference on Reconstruction. The post–Second World War era of the welfare state and the Keynesian consensus on maintaining economic equilibrium placed huge new demands on Canadian governments – demands, as the Rowell–Sirois Commission had clearly understood, which no province had sufficient control over taxation or finance to meet.

King introduced at the conference the Green Book, a pamphlet really, outlining a comprehensive plan to restructure Canadian federalism. King proposed, in return for continued provincial concessions on income and corporate taxes, a taxation and social security scheme that would give the central government the financial power and legislative authority to help the economy through depression and to institute social insurance schemes to ensure against disease, old age, and extended unemployment.

The prime minister knew that he had the support of Liberal premiers from the Maritimes, Manitoba, and British Columbia, together with CCF premier Tommy Douglas from Saskatchewan. He faced, however, implacable opposition from Quebec's premier Maurice Duplessis and Ontario's premier George Drew. Ultimately, at the last session of the conference in April 1946, Drew denounced centralization and the socialist threat of health insurance. Duplessis made the by-now-familiar arguments for provincial autonomy and compared the Dominion proposals to the work of Hitler and Mussolini. With the collapse of the conference, Ottawa then offered "tax rental" to the provinces, whereby the federal government would completely occupy the fields of income, corporation, and "succession taxes"; in return the provinces would receive a payment based on a complicated formula designed to provide both a per-capita grant and their statutory subsidies under the BNA Act. All provinces except Quebec and Ontario accepted the federal terms. Ontario and Quebec re-established their own autonomous taxation systems in 1947.

Duplessis justified Quebec's refusal to participate on the grounds that the proposals constituted an unwarranted attack on the autonomy of Quebec. While most provinces agreed that such financial co-operation was essential for the economic well-being of the whole country, Quebec saw the acceptance of grants in lieu of taxation as a sign of weakness and dependency. According to the increasingly popular orthodoxy among Quebec elites, if residents of Quebec began to look beyond their borders for assistance, their loyalty within would be weakened. No matter how many arguments were made that subsidies have always existed in the Constitution, that they were an integral part of the 1867 agreement and not destructive of provincial autonomy, Quebec nationalists distinguished between the circumstances of 1867 (and the weakness of the original provinces) and the current time, and stressed repeatedly the need for provincial fiscal autonomy in order to ensure the survival of the French language and culture in Quebec.

Meanwhile, the bricks of the welfare state continued to be laid and, with the passage of years, the federal–provincial climate on social security slowly improved. The Douglas government in Saskatchewan established Canada's first universal compulsory system of hospital insurance effective January 1, 1947. About a year later, the Liberal–Conservative coalition government in British Columbia made its own attempt, but produced chaos. Leslie Frost, who succeeded George Drew as premier of Ontario, proved to be a more flexible and moderate spokesman for Ontario in many significant respects. He got along well with federal Justice minister (later prime minister) Louis St. Laurent, and negotiated Ontario's acceptance of the tax-rental agreements in 1952. Then, in 1955, Frost actually initiated a public campaign to push the federal government into a national hospital insurance scheme. Ottawa, under pressure from National Health and Welfare minister Paul Martin, Sr. – father of the current federal Finance minister – accepted the challenge. In 1957, Martin introduced the Hospital Insurance and Diagnostic Services Act to the House of Commons, where it passed unanimously.

Most important constitutionally, in 1951 a new Old Age Pension regime was born, replacing the anemic and much-criticized joint federal–provincial pension scheme established in 1927 (which Quebec had waited until 1936 to join). Perhaps surprisingly, all provinces agreed to the necessary constitutional amendment (Section 94A of the Constitution Act, 1867) to establish a universal pension for Canadians age seventy and over, and a means-tested pension for those aged sixty-five to sixty-nine, with special Old Age Security taxes enacted to pay for the new system.

The 1951 amendment gave the Parliament of Canada the power to legislate for old age pensions. It also provided for a new constitutional principle. Until 1951, the Agriculture and Immigration power in the 1867 act was the only provision providing for concurrent (both federal and provincial) jurisdiction, and the Constitution stated clearly that, in the event of a conflict, federal law would prevail. This is known as "federal paramountcy," and it was consistent with the 1867 desire to create a strong, coherent, federal government. In contrast, the pensions amendment provided that any federal law "shall not affect the operation of any law, present or future, of a provincial legislature in relation to old age pensions" – in other words, "provincial paramountcy." For the first time in Canadian constitutional history, a matter deemed to be within federal competence was made subordinate to provincial law – presaging developments to come. Provincialists were ecstatic. It was seen as an important precedent.

In the minds of some politicians and constitutional scholars, this amendment added more "asymmetry" to the Canadian Constitution, since potentially there can be several different provincial pension schemes. Thus the amendment justifies still more "asymmetrical arrangements" to come, with different provinces as may be required. However – and the distinction is important – the amendment conferred no asymmetry with respect to legislative powers: all provinces remained equal. While it is true that Quebec runs its own pension plan, nothing prevents any of the other provinces from following the Quebec example. Moreover, as will be seen, Quebec's plan is fortunately co-ordinated with that of the rest of Canada.

Nevertheless, the argument that provincial paramountcy will prevent effective national action in numerous areas is persuasive. If provinces can override federal legislation in more and more areas, serious questions would exist concerning the legitimacy of that province's federal MPs to vote on national matters over which their provincial governments, within their provincial boundaries, now had complete control. Clearly, it may be argued that the pensions amendment *was* an unfortunate precedent and that extreme care should be taken in future before further areas of concurrent powers with provincial paramountcy are introduced into the Constitution. Despite numerous proposals over the years from provincial governments and supporters of more provincial powers to specify new areas of public policy as being "federal but subject to provincial paramountcy," the precedent has not been repeated.

Writing in the 1950s, F.R. Scott argued that the shift toward increasing provincial autonomy meant national inactivity. He had witnessed the difficulty experienced by the federal government during the Depression in establishing the badly needed unemployment scheme. He was aware, too, that the refusal of Quebec and Ontario to go along with the postwar taxation agreements was the reason cited by Ottawa for its inability to proceed with the more elaborate social-security provisions outlined in the Marsh Report and offered to the provinces at the failed 1945 Dominion–Provincial Conference.

Scott and like-minded thinkers in the postwar period, who were largely responsible for spurring governments toward what we now know as the "welfare state," were very clear about their belief in the need for a strong national government in the social and economic fields. As Scott wrote: "Laws dealing with corporations, workers' compensation, minimum wages, labour laws, industrial standards, pensions, public health, traffic regulation, collective bargaining, rent control and so forth have a common content throughout Canada because they confront common social and economic situations."

Today, as Canadians face serious social and economic dislocations, the same debate over the role of the federal government is taking place. This time, however, there are few vocal champions of the pan-Canadian cause either outside government – a marked shortage of Scotts – or within it. Years of separatist and decentralist intimidation have induced former proponents of a strong national government to hide, and fiscal conservatives have convinced others that Ottawa's debt precludes proactiveness.

In 1957 the tax rental system was placed on a new basis, now referred to as "equalization." This was the predecessor of the current system and aimed at a redistribution of revenues to alleviate the fiscal needs of poorer provinces. The initial formula was as follows: A province was allowed to collect 10 per cent of the federal personal income tax, 10 per cent of taxable corporation income, and 50 per cent of federal succession duties. Then an average was taken of the amounts to be collected by Ontario and British Columbia, the two wealthiest provinces, and grants to the remaining provinces were "equalized" in order to bring them up to that level. All provinces agreed to the new arrangement, including Quebec. But when Quebec had begun to levy its own separate income tax in 1954, Duplessis had already convinced St. Laurent to agree to reduce Quebec residents' federal tax by 10 per cent to accommodate the new provincial tax.

Following the election of the Conservative government of John Diefenbaker in 1957, the Dominion–Provincial Conference of 1960 tried to work out a new plan for sharing tax fields. Deadlock after deadlock ensued. Finally, Diefenbaker told the provinces what would happen when the five-year tax-rental agreements expired on March 31, 1962. Equalization grants, he announced, would be calculated on a somewhat different basis, subject to a "stabilization" guarantee that no province's revenue would fall by more than 5 per cent as a result of the new calculations. Adjustment grants were continued and increased. Ottawa then set the abatement in the three shared tax fields – one half of succession duties, 9 per cent of corporation income taxes, and a rising share of income tax (from 16 per cent of federal tax in 1962 to 20 per cent in 1967). This meant that the provinces had equivalent "room" to impose taxes at their own rates as long as they calculated their tax as a percentage of the federal tax. Ottawa then collected the tax on behalf of the provinces.

This system of income tax continues to the present day. Since 1962, however, the provinces have demanded more and more "tax room" and have got their way. The abatements became larger in 1963, when the Liberals under Lester Pearson returned to power, and have increased many times since then. Indeed the share of national tax revenues retained by the federal government has fallen from over 70 per cent after the First World War to barely one-third. This is the lowest such proportion of any central government in the OECD (Organization for Economic Co-operation and Development) and supports the view that Canada is one of the most decentralized federations in the world.

The equalization formula determining the unconditional grants for poorer provinces has been altered many times. The formula now involves more than thirty different sources of revenue, and the transfers contribute considerably to the revenues of the so-called have-not provinces.

THE CONSTITUTION:
(1) COMPACT THEORY REVISITED

At the same time as Duplessis forcefully pressed Quebec's financial autonomy, he was also pressing the nationalist agenda on other fronts. As has been noted earlier, since Confederation there has been a small but forceful line of thinking, primarily but not exclusively among French Canadians, that the BNA Act was a compact or treaty, meaning Ottawa is the "creature" of the provinces who agreed in 1867 to set up a new form of government. A variant of this theory holds that Confederation was a fundamental agreement, not merely between provinces, but between the two founding groups, French and English. Thus, the main influence that shaped the 1867 Constitution was said to be the French–English relationship. F.R. Scott commented on this perspective in 1957:

> There exists a dualism in the Constitution reflecting a predominant fact of Canadian life, and the government of Quebec at once appears as a "French" and "Catholic" government, a champion of the race, set

over against the English Protestant government of
Ottawa. . . . This concentration on the provincial
government as defender and sole representative of
Quebec's rights, as distinct from merely regarding the
province as a focus of culture, is something relatively
new in Quebec, though the ideas being defended are as
old as the cession of 1763.

The 1956 Duplessis-appointed Royal Commission on
Constitutional Problems (the Tremblay Commission) was
charged with examining the "encroachments" of the federal
government into the field of direct taxation, especially its
taxes on revenue, corporations, and inheritances; the consequences of these "encroachments" for the legislative and
administrative system of Quebec and for the collective,
family, and individual life of its population; and, generally,
the constitutional problems of a fiscal character. The commission's four-volume report supported the view that the
federal government was a creation of the provinces and that
the purpose of the political regime of 1867 was merely to
establish a framework within which English and French
communities could live in a federal state. It called for greater
provincial autonomy, proposing among other things that
social programs be under provincial jurisdiction. It also proposed major fiscal reforms very different from those recommended by the Rowell–Sirois report. Notably, its second
recommendation stated: "With regard to French Canadian
culture, the province of Quebec assumes alone the responsibilities which the other provinces jointly assume with regard
to Anglo-Canadian culture."

F.R. Scott, among others, attacked the Tremblay
Commission's conclusions:

> What would surprise the Canadian from Nova Scotia
> or Alberta ... is the notion that Ottawa speaks for all the
> other "English" provinces as well as for itself, and that
> because the population of Quebec is predominantly
> French and Catholic, all provinces except Quebec dis-
> appear, leaving only two "states" on the Canadian scene.

The "dual state theory" required that Quebec alone be the exclusive defender of French culture – disregarding all French minorities in other provinces. It was this historically dubious conclusion that led to intensifying demands by Quebec for more legislative powers in the postwar period. It is worth noting that the very provincial autonomy which Quebec was seeking served to further erode the rights of French-speaking minorities outside Quebec. Provincial autonomy simply strengthened the English-speaking majorities in the nine other provinces, along with their resistance to the claims of French-speaking minorities for linguistic and educational protection.

Despite Duplessis' parochial focus on Quebec, there was still a significant group of French Canadians in Quebec who shared and continued to support the pan-Canadian vision of Henri Bourassa. They recognized the importance of the survival of the French language and culture throughout Canada. In 1954, the then-publisher of *Le Devoir*, Gérard Filion, for one, pointed to the inequalities in the school system as one of the great causes of friction between the English and the French, adding: "On the day when every French Canadian, wherever he may be in the country, enjoys the same advantages and the same privileges as his English-speaking compatriot, the last obstacle to the unity of the country will have disappeared."

Duplessis ignored this argument. He continued his Quebec-first battles, notably in the broad areas of "education" and "culture." Consider, for example, the federal government's response to the 1951 Report of the Royal Commission on National Development in the Arts, Letters and Sciences (the Massey Commission). Ottawa initiated a scheme of subsidization for all universities based on a formula equally applied in all provinces. All Quebec universities accepted the plan and, initially, a special committee appointed by the Quebec government supervised the distribution of the funds. A year later, however, the Duplessis government suddenly refused further participation in the scheme and declared that the subsidies were an invasion of the province's exclusive jurisdiction over education. It then commenced its own payments, and demanded more taxing power under the Constitution to finance them, which led to the first constitutional "opting out" mechanism. In 1959 the federal government stopped direct funding of Quebec universities and gave Quebec an increased abatement of corporate income tax.

The demands then edged into the amorphous realm of "culture." The defenders of provincial autonomy, especially in Quebec, began arguing that "culture" was part of "education," and subject, therefore, to provincial jurisdiction. This, of course, ignored the fact that the courts (including the Judicial Committee of the Privy Council, in a moment of clarity) had already allocated radio and television broadcasting to the federal jurisdiction. Nonetheless, strong Quebec opposition, in particular, initially prevented the establishment of the Canada Council for the Encouragement of the Arts, Letters, Humanities and Social Sciences, recommended in the Massey Report. Yet, as the Massey Report had said: "If the federal government is to renounce its right to associate itself with other social groups, public and private, in the general education of Canadian citizens, it denies its intellectual and moral purpose, the complete conception of the common good is lost, and Canada, as such, becomes a materialistic society." Eventually, the government of Louis St. Laurent created the Canada Council in 1957.

At about the same time, Duplessis legislated an amendment to make the French text of the Civil Code and statutes of Quebec prevail over the English text, in case of conflicts. This so obviously was in breach of Section 133 of the Constitution Act, 1867 that he was persuaded to repeal the law before it was struck down by the courts.

More positively, in the early postwar period, federal control over broadcasting cemented the status of the French language outside Quebec. The Crown-owned Canadian Broadcasting Corporation set up French-language stations on the prairies, and radio and television generally were accepted as important means of extending the French language throughout all of Canada and the English language within Quebec.

THE CONSTITUTION:
(2) TIPTOEING INTO RIGHTS AND PATRIATION
John Diefenbaker, the federal prime minister of the early 1960s and a legendary trial lawyer, had a strong interest in constitutional matters.

In 1960, he secured the parliamentary passage of the Canadian Bill of Rights. Because he was unable to reach provincial agreement for a constitutional amendment entrenching his Bill of Rights, it was passed as a simple federal statute, and therefore – popular as it was among the people – it was no more than ordinary law, subject to change by any future Parliament, and it did not apply in areas of provincial jurisdiction. Nonetheless, it represented a significant effort to put certain basic rights into law.

In the same year, Jean Lesage and his Liberals took over Quebec government from the Union Nationale. At his first federal–provincial conference in July 1960, Lesage put con-stitutional reform squarely on the table. First, he demanded that the Prime Minister attempt to get agreement on a domestic amending formula so that the Constitution could finally be patriated from Britain. Second, he urged the adop-tion in the Constitution of a charter of fundamental rights, including the linguistic and educational rights of French-speaking minorities outside Quebec. He also called for an end to shared-cost programs and for appropriate compensa-tion to be paid to the provinces. He set an ultimatum for the transfer of fiscal resources to Quebec. And it should be noted that the Quebec government, in all this, did not demand many new powers – it mainly wanted more money.

In response, Diefenbaker's Justice minister, E. Davey Fulton, proposed a patriation formula (the Fulton Formula). It provided that the Constitution was to be amendable by federal law but that no law relating to the legislative powers of a province, the assets of a province, the privileges of a province, the use of the English and French languages, the determination of representation by province in the House of Commons, or the amending formula itself, was to go into effect unless it was concurred in by all provinces. It pro-vided further that no law affecting other provisions of the Constitution should come into effect unless it was con-curred in by the legislatures of at least two-thirds of the provinces, representing at least 50 per cent of the population; that no law in relation to one or more provinces (but not all provinces) should come into effect unless accepted by each province concerned; and that no law in relation to education should come into force unless concurred in by all provinces other than Newfoundland (a law amending education in that province was not to come into effect except with the consent of that province.) The formula also included the "delegation" clause, permitting provinces to delegate powers to Parliament, and vice versa (four provinces together could ask for a federal power, and Ottawa could consent).

Quebec rejected the Fulton Formula because it did not give the provinces greater powers. In general, Quebec politicians took the position that there could be no settlement of the amending formula until they were satisfied with the division of powers.

THE CONSTITUTION:
(3) "OPTING OUT" JOINS THE LANGUAGE
In 1963, Canadians elected a Liberal government led by Lester Pearson. He supported Premier Lesage's demand for the right to "opt out" of certain established programs. Quebec had already opted out of the subsidization of universities, and this provision was now continued into subsequent federal arrangements for post-secondary education. In 1964, the federal government established the Canada Student Loan Plan and offered all provinces the alternative of a direct payment to the province if it operated a similar program. Quebec immediately took up the option (as did the Northwest Territories in 1988). In the same year,

the federal government established a schooling allowance program for sixteen- and seventeen-year-olds attending school or college, similar to a program already established in Quebec in 1961. The program complemented the federal family allowances, which stopped at age sixteen. Quebec opted out of the federal scheme in exchange for a transfer of three points of basic federal income tax, which was compensation for what would have been paid under the federal program.

In 1965, Pearson passed the Established Programs Act permitting provinces to opt out of federal–provincial cost-sharing arrangements for hospital insurance and welfare, and to receive financial compensation in the form of an abatement of tax points. Only Quebec took full advantage of the mechanism, but any thought here of Quebec's "special status" was technically not an issue since all provinces could potentially have used the mechanism.

Pearson also moved ahead quickly with the introduction of the Canada Pension Plan. In response, at the federal–provincial conference in 1964, Lesage shocked the gathering by presenting a complete proposal for Quebec's own pension plan which was more generous than the federal scheme, taking the federal government completely by surprise and leaving the conference in disarray. An arrangement was hastily worked out by which Ottawa adopted Quebec's plan as parallel to its own and accepted the right of all provinces to establish their own plans, once again to avoid the appearance of special status for Quebec. (Quebec's move was, of course, entirely constitutional in light of the "provincial paramountcy" provision for pensions incorporated in Section 94A.)

To say that Lesage was pleased with all these developments would be an understatement. Quebec had secured its own pension plan. It had obtained Ottawa's commitment to Quebec's opting out of other shared-cost programs. It had, as well, negotiated a larger share of personal income tax revenues for all provinces.

Lesage felt confident enough to reject, in 1964, yet another domestic amending formula, the Fulton–Favreau Formula. Guy Favreau was Pearson's Justice minister. The Fulton–Favreau Formula modified the Fulton Formula by giving every province a veto over any change in the division of powers – in many ways the most decentralizing proposal to date. Lesage was pressured by more radical Quebec nationalists into rejecting it precisely because it gave equal powers to all provinces, which was seen as a weakening of Quebec's voice.

ENTER THREE WISE MEN: ALARUMS FOLLOWED BY RENÉ

Pearson was aware of his government's weakness in confronting Quebec's nationalists and he was personally growing tired of the battle. He decided to strengthen the influence of Quebec federalists in Ottawa and, to this end, he recruited three of the province's brightest young federalists to the Liberal party: Jean Marchand, the Quebec labour leader; Gérard Pelletier, a respected writer and thinker; and Pierre Elliott Trudeau, a legal scholar and author. All three were persuaded to run in the 1965 federal election, and all quickly assumed cabinet posts in the second Pearson government, Trudeau taking on the important Justice portfolio.

The presence of the so-called Three Wise Men was soon felt in the national capital. The Pearson government was seen to be no longer simply reacting to events in Quebec; it was taking the initiative in a wide range of areas.

For a start, in April 1966, the Prime Minister announced that all future university graduates joining the federal civil service must be bilingual or willing to become so. The background to this: In 1963 the Royal Commission on Bilingualism and Biculturalism had been created after polls showed that one in six Quebeckers saw separation as a viable option. Co-headed by André Laurendeau, editor of *Le Devoir*, and A. Davidson Dunton, former head of the CBC, its purpose was to listen to Canadians and to convince them that French had to be an equal national language. On a political level, the commission sought to convince Canadians that unless Quebeckers could be persuaded that all Canada was their homeland, the country was in serious danger of breaking up. With the 1965 report of the Bilingualism and Biculturalism Commission, the commitment to bilingualism as a concrete way to make French Canadians feel more at home and secure within Canada, not just Quebec, was made very clear.

During the 1966 federal–provincial conference, the new federal Finance minister, Mitchell Sharp, announced that the federal government would no longer "make room" for the provinces by turning over tax points. Also, shared-cost programs would be reduced in scope – a device to reduce Quebec's effective (but non-constitutional) special status arising from its opting out of major programs such as the Canada Pension Plan and the Canada Assistance Plan.

The Quebec government reacted. The Union Nationale was returned to power in 1966 under the leadership of

Daniel Johnson. Johnson demanded the restructuring of Canada as two national states as well as the acquisition by Quebec of an international personality. He appointed a Minister of Intergovernmental Affairs to "co-ordinate" Quebec's dealings with "foreign governments," a move awkwardly legitimated by Ottawa with the conclusion of an umbrella Canada–France agreement permitting governmental "contacts" at the "subnational level."

As the national excitement of the centennial year washed over the country, French president Charles de Gaulle arrived. After disembarking from a French warship below the cliffs of Quebec City and travelling along the old Chemin du Roy to Montreal, he addressed a throng from the balcony of Montreal's city hall, where he cried out: "Vive Montréal. Vive le Québec. Vive le Québec libre!" Quebec nationalists were ecstatic. The federal government was outraged and promptly rebuked de Gaulle, who abruptly ended his visit. By the end of 1967, René Lévesque, a rising star in the Quebec Liberal party, split from the Liberals to create a united Mouvement Souveraineté-Association, out of which was formed – in 1969 – a single Parti Québécois.

CHAPTER 5

TRUDEAU AND THE VISION RECAST

Canada seemed to me to be an ideal country for a policy of greater equality of opportunity. A young country, a rich country, a country of two languages, of ethnic and religious plurality and of federative structure. Canada also possessed a political tradition that was neither entirely libertarian nor entirely socialist, but rested on an indispensable partnership between government and the private sector, and on direct action by the state to protect the weak from the strong, the disadvantaged from the well-heeled.

— Pierre Trudeau, *Towards a Just Society*

PIERRE ELLIOTT TRUDEAU entered federal politics as a candidate for the Liberal party on November 5, 1965, citing – in the last article he wrote for the magazine he co-founded, *Cité Libre* – Plato's aphorism that the price for those who stay out of politics is to be governed by people worse than themselves. The Constitution, when he arrived in Ottawa as a newly elected MP, was not high on his list of priorities, although he had clearly set out his views on the need for a constitutional charter of rights.

Like Louis St. Laurent (prime minister from 1948 to 1957 and an outstanding constitutional lawyer), Trudeau believed the provinces had enough power to shape their own destinies and that demands for more power and money were designed simply to benefit provincial elites and provincial bureaucracies. Like Henri Bourassa, who sixty years earlier had taken up the cause of French-speaking minorities outside Quebec and had urged French-speaking Quebeckers to look beyond their province's borders, Trudeau strongly believed that the survival of French-speaking Canadians was better assured in the wider Canadian context. The federal government, he said, spoke legitimately for French-speaking Canadians; at most one could say that Quebec was the predominant repository of French Canadians within North America.

His priorities were soon adjusted by political events, by no means least among them French president Charles de Gaulle's declaration from the balcony of Montreal city hall. ("Ca allait accélerer beaucoup de choses," – "This will speed up a lot of things" – noted René Lévesque, then still a provincial Liberal deputy, who was present in the crowd.) As Canadians awakened to the fact that their country was in danger of disintegrating, so, too, did they become aware that Pierre Trudeau was remarkably suited to meet that threat. His appointment as Prime Minister Lester Pearson's parliamentary secretary drew a protest from Quebec premier Jean Lesage, irritated by the recognition shown to such a vocal opponent of the argument for special status.

Lesage's Union Nationale successor, Daniel Johnson, published a book in 1965 titled *Egalité ou indépendence* which his party adopted as policy. The book was the compact theory refreshed and amplified. Trudeau mocked the idea as a hoax, a practical joke. In his first major speech as Justice minister in 1967, he advocated the entrenchment in a patriated constitution of both linguistic rights and individual human rights. That, he said, was the path to making Canada modern, the path to a renewed federalism. Johnson argued that Ottawa's power over Quebec had to be diminished, that Quebec had to be given equal power to English-speaking Canada in directing the central government, and that, if those conditions were not met, Quebec would be compelled to become an independent state. Beyond Quebec's borders, the "equality" proposition was not taken seriously. However, other provincial premiers, notably Ontario's John Robarts, supported Quebec's desire for a diminished federal government and, together, by means of the Confederation for Tomorrow conference in November 1967, they persuaded Prime Minister Pearson to convene a federal–provincial constitutional conference in February 1968.

THE FIRST STEP: LANGUAGE

Pearson, at seventy, was tired of politics and eager to pass the baton to a francophone successor with a solution to the separatist threat. On February 5, he nervously opened the conference, reminding those assembled that the country's future was at stake and hoping that the issue would be addressed delicately and diplomatically. Instead, his Justice minister and Quebec's premier squared off against each other before a national television audience, with Trudeau eloquently and triumphantly winning the exchange. The forcefulness of his arguments, and the poise and confidence which he displayed at the conference, were crucial elements to his election as Liberal leader a few months later and his subsequent victory at the polls with a large national majority.

The first Trudeau government set about changing the image of Ottawa as a government dominated by anglophones. It encouraged French Canadians to participate in the federal government, to believe in federal institutions. It took steps to ensure that Quebeckers and other French-speaking Canadians could feel at home in every part of Canada. The Official Languages Act, passed in 1969, was a major step in this direction.

The act, intended as the cornerstone of the government's new constitutional edifice, broadened the scope and application of Section 133 of the BNA Act. Its purpose was to give English and French equal status not only in Parliament and the courts of Canada, as required by Section 133, but also throughout the federal administration. It created an arm's-length watchdog, the Commissioner of Official Languages, to promote the act's objectives.

Contrary to much that was said in opposition to the Official Languages Act, it forced no one to learn or to speak French against his or her will; indeed, it placed no obligations at all upon Canadian citizens. Rather, it obliged the federal government to serve and respond to Canadian citizens in the official language of a citizen's choice.

THE VICTORIA CHARTER:
SETTING AND AFTERMATH

The election of a majority Trudeau government was followed in April 1970 by the election of a Liberal government in Quebec under Robert Bourassa, a young technocrat who, unlike his predecessor, Daniel Johnson, believed that federalism could be "profitable" for Quebeckers. Sensing an opportunity to work with a Quebec premier more constitutionally moderate than Johnson, Trudeau reopened negotiations with the provinces on language rights, on a constitutionally entrenched bill of rights, on the division of powers, and on a Canadian amending formula that would allow for the Constitution's final patriation from Britain.

The context of that time is important. Political unrest in Quebec, particularly in respect of language issues, was intensifying. In November and December 1969, there had been bombings in Montreal. Terrorists of the Front de Libération du Québec (FLQ) had been increasingly active. In October 1970, they kidnapped British trade commissioner James Cross. A few days later, another FLQ cell kidnapped Quebec Labour minister Pierre Laporte.

In the Quebec National Assembly, the Parti Québécois opposition urged Bourassa to form a coalition government and defy Ottawa by negotiating with the FLQ for the release of the two hostages. Bourassa, under pressure from the Trudeau government to maintain a united front, refused. He did, however, request the federal government to declare the War Measures Act, stating that an "apprehended insurrection" was taking place in Quebec, and giving the police extraordinary powers of arrest and detention. The police interpreted their mandate excessively, arresting and detaining more than four hundred persons, although the federal cabinet had originally been shown a list of only seventy suspects. At one point, police entered the home of the federal Secretary of State, Gérard Pelletier, in search of another person of the same name, having relied on a telephone book for the suspect's address. With the murder of Pierre Laporte on October 17 and the release of Cross in December, the "October Crisis" ended. No "insurrection" had found purchase in Quebec, and the FLQ thereafter appeared to disintegrate. The debate may never end over whether the imposition of the War Measures Act was justified, although it was passed by Parliament with nearly unanimous support, and enjoyed overwhelming public support in both French-speaking and English-speaking Canada. Quebec nationalists added it to their list of wrongs imposed by Ottawa to justify the push for independence.

What came to be called the Victoria Charter emerged in 1971 from federal–provincial negotiations held in Victoria, B.C. While some concessions were made in respect of the provinces' demands for more powers, significant steps were taken to promote the bilingual character of Canada, to entrench a bill of rights, and to patriate the Constitution. The bill of rights provisions were quite modest, entrenching only a limited number of fundamental freedoms subject to "such limitations . . . as are reasonably justifiable in a democratic society in the interests of public safety, order, health or morals, of national security, or of the rights and freedoms of others." The latter clause was so porous that, to use the popular aphorism, a Mack truck could be driven through it.

In contrast, the agreement with respect to language rights was quite extensive. The use of French was to be guaranteed in Parliament and in all provincial legislatures except those of Saskatchewan, Alberta, and British Columbia (which did not accept the stipulation). French would be used in federal courts, and in provincial courts in New Brunswick, Newfoundland, and Quebec. An individual had the right to choose which official language to use in communications between him- or herself and the head or central office of every department and agency of the government of Canada and the provincial governments of Ontario, Quebec, New Brunswick, Prince Edward Island, and Newfoundland.

Provincial participation would be permitted in the nomination of Supreme Court judges, and any case involving the Quebec Civil Code would be heard by a panel consisting of a majority of judges from Quebec. Ottawa would concede provincial supremacy under the Constitution's division of powers in such social policy matters as family, youth, and occupational training allowances and would add those fields to Section 94A of the Constitution Act, 1867 (which dealt with pensions), thereby expanding the areas of joint jurisdiction subject to provincial paramountcy.

Finally, there was an amending formula based on four regions – the Atlantic provinces, the West, Quebec, and Ontario. For most constitutional amendments, the formula required the consent of the federal Parliament and any province that had at any time 25 per cent of the population of Canada (Ontario and Quebec alone would qualify), and at least two of the four Atlantic provinces, and at least two of the four Western provinces with a combined population of 50 per cent of the West. This gave Ontario and Quebec an effective veto over constitutional change. A federal initiative to include a referendum as a deadlock-breaking device was rejected. Yet a referendum mechanism would have provided a safeguard against any provincial government acting contrary to the wishes of the majority of the population by refusing to consent to an amendment. Its absence – then and now – leads to confusion over the *real* source of sovereignty in Canada: the *people* or some combination of their federal and provincial governments.

Since the Victoria Charter conference, a number of federal proposals (including those in the 1982 amendments) to include a referendum mechanism in the amending formula have been blocked by provincial governments. The popular revulsion toward the Meech Lake exercise – in which the first ministers unsuccessfully tried to force through significant constitutional amendments without testing public support – shows the strength of Canadians' feelings that the Constitution belongs to the people. The Charlottetown referendum vindicated this feeling. Indeed, the Charlottetown referendum may have established a constitutional convention requiring a referendum before any significant constitutional change is made.

Bourassa certainly had not achieved everything he had wanted at the Victoria negotiations, but he accepted their result. He subsequently was so castigated by Claude Castonguay, his Minister of Social Affairs, and publicly by Claude Ryan, the influential editor of *Le Devoir*, for coming away with so little in the way of new legislative powers – especially on income security and social services – that he meekly withdrew his consent and refused to ask his government to approve it. The Victoria Charter passed into history.

LANGUAGE WARS AND DEUX NATIONS

The next major confrontation between Ottawa and Quebec came with Bourassa's enactment of Bill 22 in 1974. French was declared the only official language of Quebec. English-language schools were restricted primarily to those whose maternal language was English, and incentives were put in place for firms to expand the use of French in their daily operations ("francization"), and in their dealings with customers.

While Trudeau disliked Bill 22, he rejected proposals that he use the power of disallowance to invalidate the legislation* or to refer it to the Supreme Court to determine its constitutionality. He argued that the federal Parliament should not disallow a provincial law simply because it was foolish and unjust. However, having sidestepped this potential federal–provincial dispute, the federal government then bungled an opportunity to expand the use of French in air-traffic control by making several airports in Quebec bilingual. When airline pilots went on strike in June 1976, claiming the use of French would compromise "air safety," the government capitulated to English-Canadian pressure to keep English as the only language of air-control. Federalist support in Quebec was seriously undermined. When the provincial Liberal government was defeated by René Lévesque's Parti Québécois in November 1976, Bourassa singled out the airport-language dispute as an important contributing factor.

Canada's constitution industry was catapulted into overdrive with the PQ victory. Academics fell over one another – as they would a decade later – to come up with solutions to this new national crisis. A common thread in their recommendations was proposals for massive decentralization of government powers and the recognition of the compact theory of Confederation, however inaccurate the theory continued to be.

One variant of the theory – "deux nations" – had gained currency in the period after Jean Lesage was elected Quebec premier and Quebec politicians began to refer to Quebec as a "nation." The "deux nations" theory labelled Quebec as a

---

* Under Section 90, Constitution Act, 1867. In 1981, the Supreme Court said, *obiter*, that "disallowance of provincial legislation, although in law still open, [has] to all intents and purposes fallen into disuse."

nation somehow co-equal with the nation of English-speaking Canadians in the rest of the country. This was hesitantly accepted by the federal Progressive Conservative party in the 1968 election campaign (led by Robert Stanfield) in an unsuccessful attempt to attract Quebec support.

Like the compact theory, "deux nations" reflected the idea that the federal government and, indeed, the Canadian federal state, had little legitimacy of its own, and was simply the product of a pact, in this case between two nations. One of Stanfield's successors, Brian Mulroney, was clearly inspired by this theory in his later constitutional initiatives. For a brief period during the Charlottetown referendum campaign, some well-meaning but misguided Canadians even tried to extend the idea to embrace "three nations" in order to accommodate the aspirations of aboriginal Canadians.

Some of the assumptions of the compact theory were reflected in the report of Task Force on Canadian Unity. Known as the Pépin–Robarts committee after its co-chairmen, former federal minister Jean-Luc Pépin and former Ontario Conservative premier John Robarts, the committee was established by Ottawa in 1977 in response to the election of the PQ. It recommended, among other things: that language rights be left to provincial jurisdiction rather than be entrenched in the Constitution; that the Senate be replaced by a Council of the Federation appointed by the provinces; that the provinces be given power to rule on federal appointments to the Supreme Court; and that federal powers be reduced except in the area of economic management. Trudeau simply ignored the task force, sticking to his belief in a strong federal government in which Quebeckers would be as active as they were in their provincial government. In the elections of 1972, 1974, and 1979, Quebec voters supported his vision of Canada and his pan-Canadian approach to the promotion of the French language.

The new Quebec premier, René Lévesque, introduced Bill 101 – a successor to Bourassa's Bill 22 language law. English-language education was further restricted – access was guaranteed to children of parents who had themselves been educated in English in Quebec and to younger brothers and sisters of children already enrolled in English language schools; but that was it. The children of all immigrants, including immigrants from other provinces, had to attend French-language schools. Businesses had to institute programs of francization. Signs had to be French only. The Office de la Langue Française wrote and enforced these regulations. The office's "language police" were nothing if not vigilant. When a contraband shipment of English-only Dunkin' Donuts bags was uncovered, it was burned by the authorities.

Quebec anglophones argued, publicly and unsuccessfully, that in protecting the language of the majority against imagined terrors, the Parti Québécois was negating the basic individual rights of a minority of one million persons. And while it was certainly true that the anglophone provinces had not treated their French-speaking minorities very well, it was also true that New Brunswick and Ontario were expanding French-language rights in the 1970s and 1980s, and that the number of children in French immersion classes across the country was steadily rising.

PQ SEEKS SOVEREIGNTY-ASSOCIATION, INTENTIONS SERIOUS

In November 1979, Lévesque issued a thirty-thousand-word White Paper outlining his government's proposal for sovereignty-association with the rest of Canada, to be voted on in a province-wide referendum. The White Paper set out Quebec's history within Canada in a compendium of historical inaccuracies, which included:

- In 1914 despite firm and virtually unanimous opposition (from Quebec), Canada entered the war. (In fact, opposition was muted in Quebec – Henri Bourassa initially supported the war – and not restricted to Quebec.)
- The National Policy of 1879, which protected Canadian manufacturing, benefited only Ontario. (In fact, it probably benefited Quebec more.)
- Ottawa had been engaged in a "formidable centralizing attack" on the provinces since the Second World War, an attack that was intensifying. (The allegation was unsubstantiated.)

The White Paper assured the electorate there would be no sovereignty without association. It proposed four Quebec–Canada agencies: a community council, a commission of experts, a court of justice, and a monetary authority. Although the other provincial premiers warned that association would not be so easy, Lévesque told every audience the provinces would come around "on their knees" if there was a popular mandate for sovereignty. Claude Ryan, now leader of the Quebec Liberal party, responded with his own Beige Paper published in January 1980. It was predictably provincialist – one of its major proposals was a federal council, a provincially based watchdog over a new, decentralized constitutional structure.

The referendum question was formally debated in the National Assembly and agreed to in March 1980. Its wording:

The Government of Quebec has made public its proposal to negotiate a new agreement with the rest of
Canada, based on the equality of nations; this agreement would enable Quebec to acquire the exclusive
power to make its laws, levy its taxes and establish
relations abroad – in other words, sovereignty – and
at the same time, to maintain with Canada an economic association including a common currency; no
change in political status resulting from these negotiations will be effected without approval from the
people through another referendum; on these terms,
do you give the Government of Quebec the mandate
to negotiate the proposed agreement between Quebec
and Canada?

The referendum was set for May 20, 1980. Contrary to
expectations, interventions by the once-again prime minister, Pierre Trudeau,[*] and an attachment by Quebeckers to
Canada, turned out to be much more significant factors in
the referendum campaign than bread-and-butter issues.
Polls showed that 57 per cent of francophone voters expected
that economic conditions would either improve or remain
the same if Quebec achieved sovereignty-association. But 72
per cent of francophone voters (and 96 per cent of anglophones) indicated a deep attachment to Canada. In the
result, sovereignty-association was rejected by 59.5 per cent
of voters. A majority of French Canadians (52 per cent)

---

[*] The federal Liberals were defeated in 1979 by the Conservatives led by
Joe Clark, whose minority government lost a parliamentary vote of
confidence nine months later, precipitating an election in early 1980,
which the Liberals won.

voted No, and the No vote was geographically widespread across the province. The fact that a significant proportion of francophones voting yes in the referendum also indicated a deep attachment to Canada reflects Quebeckers' chronic ambivalence about the country and confusion about the actual meaning of a separate Quebec.

RENEWED FEDERALISM:
THE PROMISE, THE OUTCOME

Throughout the 1970s, several provinces had demanded what they called constitutional "reform," which invariably meant a devolution of powers to the provinces. Each province had a shopping list. British Columbia and Newfoundland, for example, wanted control of off-shore resources. British Columbia also wanted a Senate appointed by the provinces with no federal representation. Saskatchewan and Alberta wanted control of indirect taxation, as well as more control over natural resources, including the related aspects of international trade. The Atlantic provinces wanted control over fisheries.

A committee of federal and provincial ministers did examine all these issues through the winter of 1978–79 in the hope of reaching an agreement on the division of powers, a domestic amending formula, and a charter of rights – and, by extension, the Constitution's patriation. An agreement did emerge, with a marked provincialist tilt, but it was rejected by the Quebec government (which had made clear it did not want progress made, or seen to be made, before its promised sovereignty referendum).

In the meantime, the Trudeau government in 1978 proposed a two-phase process of reform and constitutional change. As at Victoria seven years earlier, the aim was to bring the Constitution home, entrench a bill of rights, better secure French-speaking-minority rights and the bilingual character of Canada, and update the division of powers.

Phase one would revamp – update – the British North America Act (Constitution Act, 1867) in federal areas of jurisdiction by July 1, 1979, making revisions which it was argued could be implemented unilaterally by the federal government. These included putting in place a preamble to the Constitution stating the aims of the Canadian federation, entrenching a Charter of Human Rights and Freedoms applicable only to areas of federal jurisdiction, entrenching the Supreme Court of Canada and its composition, reforming the Senate by replacing it with a House of the Federation whose members would be jointly appointed by the federal and provincial governments, and vesting executive government in the governor general acting in the name of the Queen rather than in the Queen herself. Phase two, to be concluded by the fiftieth anniversary of the Statute of Westminster (July 1, 1981), would address the federal–provincial division of powers.

The federal government's proposals – introduced as Bill C-60 in the summer of 1978 – quickly became mired in political and legal controversy. All ten premiers, including René Lévesque, rejected altering the monarchy and unilateral federal reform of the Senate. The federal government agreed to refer its Senate proposal to the Supreme Court of Canada, which ruled that the Senate could not be reformed unilaterally by the federal Parliament; provincial consent was required as well.

The Trudeau government was defeated in the election of May 1979. Joe Clark – with a decentralized view of the country – became prime minister of a minority Conservative government which itself was defeated within a year, returning Trudeau and his Liberals to office with a new agenda for constitutional change.

Trudeau now proposed that, in return for various concessions to provincial demands, the "economic union" of Canada and *national* powers over the economy should be strengthened. Moreover, in addition to this "package for governments," there was to be a "package for people" – a Charter of Rights and Freedoms, the constitutional entrenchment of English and French as official languages, plus entrenchment of minority language and education rights, equalization payments from rich to poor provinces, an amending formula, and patriation. The monarchy was left alone. The new proposals from the outset smacked into a wall of competing visions of the country – with declarations by Newfoundland premier Brian Peckford, for example, that he preferred René Lévesque's vision of Canada to Trudeau's: namely, that the national government was properly the agent of the provinces.

The September 1980 first ministers' Constitution conference disintegrated in acrimony. Trudeau announced that the federal government would proceed to unilaterally patriate the Constitution. The resolution his government intended to submit to the British Parliament incorporated an amending formula with an alternative referendum mechanism; a charter of rights, including minority language and education rights; equalization; and a guarantee of national standards of public services to all Canadians. There were fifty-nine clauses in all and an appendix annexing twenty-nine other statutes to what was to be the new fundamental law of Canada.

The governments of Ontario and New Brunswick supported Trudeau; the governments of six other provinces[*]
referred the federal initiative to the courts. At the same
time, provincial governments, with Quebec's agent general
in London, Gilles Loiselle,[†] in the vanguard, began inten-
sively lobbying the British Parliament's Foreign Affairs
Committee, which had begun an inquiry into what conventions existed governing the amendment of the Canadian
Constitution. The committee, to the provinces' immense
satisfaction, concluded that the federal government had
never before unilaterally altered the distribution of powers
in the Canadian Constitution, but rather had done so only
with a substantial measure of provincial consent.

On April 16, 1981, the Gang of Six provinces, now swelled
to the Gang of Eight (all but Ontario and New Brunswick),
signed their own constitutional patriation model – the
"April Accord" – with a fanfare of publicity before the TV
cameras. In signing the accord, the government of Quebec
abandoned its claim to a veto over constitutional change by
accepting an amending formula that would permit constitutional changes with which Quebec might not agree, but
which permitted dissenting provinces to opt out of the
provisions of an amendment with financial compensation.
This was cast by Quebec's negotiators as a *de facto* veto,
because no change could ever apply to Quebec without
Quebec's consent, and no fiscal penalty would be incurred

---

[*] Nova Scotia and Saskatchewan initially were not part of the Gang of
Six but joined later.

[†] Later a Cabinet minister in the government of Brian Mulroney.
Loiselle, employing one of London's best chefs, Arturo, exquisitely wined
and dined British MPs, notably those who sat on the Foreign Affairs
Committee.

by Quebec's non-participation. The accord was immediately rejected by Trudeau.

Twelve days later, the justices of the Supreme Court of Canada began hearing arguments on the legality of unilateral federal action. On September 28, the Court delivered its judgment. It was somewhat confusing. The Court concluded that unilateral patriation would not be in accordance with constitutional convention – but would not be illegal. The federal government claimed victory, but it was clear to all the combatants that a request for patriation without substantial provincial consent would be coolly received by Britain's lawmakers.

Ottawa and the provinces – the Gang of Eight bringing with them their April Accord – returned to the negotiating table in November. There, Trudeau succeeded in cracking the provincial common front by getting Lévesque to agree to the notion of submitting a federal constitutional package (including a Charter of Rights and Freedoms) to the people of Canada in a referendum if, within two years, there was no agreement among governments. "It seems an honourable way out," Lévesque told reporters afterwards. "We've been saying all along Trudeau has no mandate from the people for this *coup de force* [unilateral action]." But the seven other premiers balked – and abandoned Quebec in what has come to be known in constitutional folklore as "the night of the long knives."

Justice minister Jean Chrétien then proceeded to negotiate a compromise general amending formula with the attorneys-general of Ontario and Saskatchewan, Roy McMurtry and Roy Romanow, which ultimately became the "general amending formula" of the final constitutional package. It contained no provision for a provincial veto.

Rather, an amendment would require the consent of Ottawa and at least seven provinces having 50 per cent of the population (the so-called 7-50 rule). Opting out of an amendment by as many as three dissenting provinces was permitted, but without fiscal compensation for doing so except in the unlikely event of an amendment awarding jurisdiction to the federal government over education and other cultural matters. The provision for opting out *without* fiscal compensation was important, because it ensured there would be an incentive for a province to agree to an amendment and *not* opt out. Opting out *with* compensation, as originally demanded by the Gang of Eight, would have made provincial dissent effectively painless and would inevitably have diminished federal leverage in any constitutional negotiation. Nonetheless, Canada is the only country in the world that makes opting out a central feature of constitutional amendment.

In addition to the general amending formula, there were two other formulas agreed to for changing the Constitution. The first addressed specific matters that would require unanimous consent of Parliament and all provincial legislatures – thereby giving each province and the federal Parliament a veto. This applied to changes to the amending formulas themselves, the composition of the Supreme Court, Canada's status as a constitutional monarchy, and the use of the English and French languages. The second formula was for amendments pertaining to only one province (for example, an amendment to the terms by which it joined Confederation), which could be made by the province involved and the federal Parliament.

Agreement on a domestic amending formula (at least between Ottawa and nine of the ten provinces – Quebec

did not accept it) cut the colonial Gordian knot tying
Canada's Constitution to the United Kingdom's Parliament.
Unfortunately the formula did not resolve the issue of
popular sovereignty. The amending formula, adapted from
the Gang of Eight's April Accord, set in place a purely intergovernmental mechanism largely insensitive to the interests
of the people of Canada, to the national community and
its national government. Again, the chance to include a referendum mechanism was lost, a chance to confirm that
ultimate sovereignty resides in Canada's *people*, not their
governments. The federal government's resolution of
October 1980 had contained a mechanism empowering
Parliament to call a referendum as an alternative to obtain-
ing the agreement of the requisite provincial governments
(with an amendment deemed to be approved if it received
the support of a national majority of voters plus a majority
from those provinces whose legislatures would otherwise
have been required to approve a proposed amendment – an
adapted Victoria Charter formula).

In addition to the general amending formula, the Charter
of Rights and Freedoms was constitutionally entrenched. To
persuade those provincial governments which disliked a
charter to come onside, a so-called notwithstanding clause
was also entrenched which allowed governments to override certain basic rights in the Charter for a five-year period
(that could be renewed) notwithstanding the Charter's protections. Those rights included the fundamental political
freedoms in Section 2, and the legal and equality rights in
Sections 7 to 15. Significantly, mobility rights and minority
language and education rights were excluded from the
override, or notwithstanding, clause.

At a press conference late in the afternoon on November 18, 1981, Trudeau was asked if this compromise agreement with the provinces had cost him a slice of his principles. Had he not bartered away people's rights to make a deal, something he had said he would never do? He replied, candidly, "Yes." The override clause saddened him, he said, because of fears that it would lead to a checkerboard Canada with some rights respected in some provinces but not in others. So, too, was he saddened by the loss of the referendum provision "so that the people's will cannot be tested." Then he said, icily "You're asking me now if I consider it a success. No, I consider it an abject failure." And he abruptly stood up and walked out of the room. The compromise resolution went to Britain's Parliament, where it was passed, and Canada's Constitution shortly thereafter came home. As the Constitution Act, 1982 it was given royal assent by the Queen at a Parliament Hill ceremony while, across the river in Quebec, flags on provincial buildings flew at half-staff.

THE IMPACT OF THE CHARTER

The Charter of Rights and Freedoms proved from the start to be immensely popular with Canadians, in Quebec as much as elsewhere. In June 1992, a decade after the Charter became part of Canada's Constitution, a CROP opinion survey found that more than 70 per cent of Quebeckers gave the Charter strong support. Political scientist Max Nemni has noted: "By linking individual civil liberties with the protection of the French language, and by enshrining the fundamental concept of two official languages, the Charter undermined

Quebeckers' major reason for pursuing the secessionist option – which was their fear of losing their language."

And yet some Quebeckers, mainly members of the nationalist elite, have argued that the Quebec government's powers have been unilaterally diminished by the Constitution Act, 1982, the implication being that the Charter in particular favours the federal government and centralism. Nothing could be more incorrect. The Charter restricts *all* the powers of government at all levels in favour of basic rights and freedoms held by all Canadians. Indeed,* the Charter of Rights and Freedoms is transforming both the general conduct of Canadian politics and the language of political discourse.

UBC political scientist Alan Cairns and others have observed that with the implementation of the Charter in 1982 – with the constitutionally entrenched protection of basic rights and freedoms against all levels of governments – Canadians now have a very real sense that their Constitution belongs to them, that it can no longer be tinkered with by the pre-1982 methods of elitist executive federalism. This lesson would be reinforced in years ahead by those first ministers who would produce the Meech Lake and Charlottetown accords. The Charter in addition has bolstered Canadians' firm belief in the equality of all citizens in Canada, which has been translated into a popular insistence on the uniform application of the Charter across Canada so that all Canadians enjoy the same rights and freedoms wherever they live.

It is a uniquely Canadian document. It is a late-twentieth-century document – positively balancing individual liberties against the authority of governments to govern for the benefit of all, rather than negatively preoccupied with limiting the authority of government, as was the case when the American Constitution was framed two hundred years earlier. In sharp contrast to the American Bill of Rights, the Charter reflects a belief that there need not be any contradiction between state regulation and individual liberty, and that freedom where appropriate is enhanced by public institutions and state action.

The Charter, for example, requires Canadians and their governments to take into account cultural, religious, linguistic, and aboriginal communities in interpreting the rights guaranteed to individuals. This allows for the protection of minorities and those individuals whose fulfilment depends on the preservation of a group identity – among them the disabled, the old, women, Canadians of all ethnic backgrounds and creeds – without undermining the ideal of a constitutionally protected equality of all citizens.

To illustrate what this means, the late constitutional scholar Walter Tarnopolsky drew the distinction between rights which all human beings possess simply by being human beings ("individual rights" or "human rights") and additional rights which individuals possess by belonging to a particular group ("group rights").

The first type of rights – individual rights – are "negative" rights, protected by requiring governments to *refrain* from interfering in people's lives. The second type of rights – group rights – are "positive," requiring governments to take action to protect individuals.

Such group rights are to be distinguished from "collective rights," in which a right is *vested* in the collectivity, not the individual. For example, an individual who is resident anywhere in Canada and who speaks either of the two official languages has the protected group right to use that language in dealing with the federal government. This right is vested in the *individual*, although he or she may decide to assert the right by voluntarily joining or forming a group of like-minded individuals.

In contrast, a constitutionalized special status for Quebec would bestow collective rights on the Quebec political entity: the "distinct society" essentially administered and regulated by the Quebec government. The Quebec government would assert these rights on behalf of individuals living in the "distinct society." Dissenting individuals would have no choice as to whether to belong to the collectivity or group (the rules of membership would be defined by the government) or whether to subscribe to the actions of the collectivity.

These unique individual rights/group rights aspects of the Charter most obviously manifest themselves in the constitutional guarantees of equality, minority language and education rights, mobility rights, and the commitment to multiculturalism, all of which are subject only to "such reasonable limits prescribed by law as can be demonstrably justified in a free and democratic society."[*] The reasonable-limits formula is a critical element in the Charter, one of many specific contrasts to the American Bill of Rights. No specific limit was originally written into the American Constitution, and it took years for the U.S. courts to develop the concept of judge-made limits on rights and freedoms that provided governments with the needed flexibility to implement, among other things, progressive social legislation.

Section 1 of the Charter has given the courts an explicit

---

[*] Section 1 of the Charter of Rights and Freedoms, Constitution Act, 1982

mandate to balance individual rights with the Canadian tradition of government action to advance Canadians' collective well-being as well as with Canada's federal diversity. Consider, for example, the case dealing with the sign law related to Quebec's Bill 101. Although in 1988, the Supreme Court of Canada ruled that banning English on outdoor signs was a breach of the Charter's Section 2(b) guarantee of freedom of expression, the Court also held that it would be permissible, under Section 1, for the Quebec government to mandate predominance of the French language on outdoor signs. The Quebec government initially rejected this option and took the regrettable step of invoking the notwithstanding clause to order a complete ban on English. It was clear, however, that a significant number of Quebeckers could have accepted the Supreme Court's position – and, indeed, a number of years later, in 1993, the Quebec government decided not to renew the notwithstanding clause and to redraft the legislation to comply with the Charter's Section 2(b) protection.

To further illustrate the unique features and impact of our Charter, it should be noted how clearly the Charter's focus on rights and fundamental values is shaping the public policy agenda. Policy makers take careful steps to "Charter-proof" proposed legislation and other government action so as to pre-empt court challenges, and groups and individuals use the Charter as their reference of principle in lobbying governments for changes to the law.

The Charter's influence is perhaps most obviously felt in public-policy areas pertaining to inequality and inequity in Canadian life, notably employment and social-assistance policies. It has created greater awareness of the needs of disadvantaged groups such as women, visible minorities, natives, the disabled. Using the Charter, steps have been taken through affirmative-action and pay-equity initiatives to improve these groups' well-being. More frequently, Canadians now speak of a person's "right" to a decent minimum standard of living, to a decent quality of life, as being as worthy of protection as traditional property rights and contractual rights.

More broadly, the Charter is having a subtle nationalizing effect, defining values and standards of national citizenship that transcend regional identity.

The step taken in 1982 to vest minority language rights in *individuals* was a great historic compromise. Historically our reliance on the benevolence of governments to protect minority rights has proven to be unwise. When, for example, the government of Ontario in the early years of the twentieth century moved to limit French as a language of instruction to the first two primary grades, then-federal opposition leader Wilfrid Laurier could do no more than plead, unsuccessfully, for a "regime of tolerance."[*] More than twenty years earlier, as prime minister, Laurier had just as unsuccessfully tried "sunny ways" to oppose the elimination of separate schools in Manitoba. The answer in 1982 was to provide members of minority language groups with legally enforceable rights that could be asserted against both federal and provincial levels of government – sharply in

---

[*] The Judicial Committee of the Privy Council ruled, in *Ottawa Roman Catholic Separate School Trustees v. Mackell* (1916), that Section 93 of the Constitution Act, 1867 did not protect language rights of French-speaking Roman Catholics on the grounds that the statutory law governing separate schools before Confederation did not confer upon them the legal right to use French as a language of instruction.

contrast to the 1867 constitutional language which had left matters in the hands of the federal government, first to decide whether provincial action *had* violated minority rights; second, to decide whether to take remedial action.[*]

The Charter's guarantees of minority language and education rights are unique for the very fact that they reflect the blend of individual rights and group identity of which Tarnopolsky spoke. Language rights do not exist in a vacuum. To allow individuals to meaningfully assert those rights, there must also be means of ensuring the preservation and promotion of linguistic communities. The language guarantees, while vested in individuals, reflect a positive rather than a negative idea of freedom by placing a positive obligation on the courts and legislatures to promote the opportunity to use and develop a citizen's language.

At the same time, individuals are free – not required – to group together to promote their collective interest. The collectivity *per se* has no rights. Thus language rights are *not* so-called collective rights. Collective rights historically have been an ideological weapon of nationalists and of the extreme Left and Right, aimed at neutralizing the liberal concern with the dignity of individuals by eliminating individual choice as to whether to be identified with one group or another. The Charter, since its inception, has been used successfully by members of francophone minorities outside of Quebec to compel provincial governments to expand the availability of French-language services and French-language education, actions that send positive signals to French Canadians in Quebec about the bilingual

---

[*] Section 93(3), Constitution Act, 1867

nature of Canada. To say the least, this is a critical compo-
nent of any long-term reconciliation of Quebec's position
within Canada.

PROMOTING EQUAL OPPORTUNITIES

In addition to the domestic amending formula and the
Charter, the 1982 constitutional reforms entrenched equalization payments (whereby rich provinces contribute to the
budgets of poor provinces) and introduced an important
clause guaranteeing comparable levels of national public
services across the country.

Section 36(2) of the Constitution Act, 1982 says:

> Parliament and the government of Canada are com-
> mitted to the principle of making equalization pay-
> ments to ensure that provincial governments have
> sufficient revenues to provide reasonably comparable
> levels of public services at reasonably comparable levels
> of taxation.

Section 36(1) says:

> Without altering the legislative authority of Parliament
> or of the provincial legislatures, or the rights of any of
> them with respect to the exercise of their legislative
> authority, Parliament and the legislatures, together
> with the government of Canada and the provincial
> governments, are committed to:

> (a)   promoting equal opportunities for the well-being
> of Canadians;

(b) furthering economic development to reduce disparity in opportunities; and
(c) providing essential services of reasonable quality
to all Canadians.

Finally, the provinces gained some additional powers in
respect of the exploitation of natural resources, electrical
energy, and forestry (Section 92A), with some important
safeguards for federal power.

WAS QUEBEC EXCLUDED?
The Quebec government refused to accept the 1982
amendments. Few expected that René Lévesque's government, committed to independence, would have done anything else. The majority of Quebec's federal members of
Parliament (seventy out of seventy-five) voted in favour
of the amendments, and polls indicated a generally wide
acceptance of them among Quebeckers. Perhaps more
revealingly, a March 1982 CROP poll reported that 48 per
cent of Quebeckers criticized Lévesque's government for
refusing to sign the accord, while only 32 per cent agreed
with its decision. Three months later, a Gallup poll reported
that 49 per cent of Quebeckers approved of the new act and
only 16 per cent disapproved. Given these findings, it is
regrettable that Trudeau was compelled to barter away the
referendum mechanism and, with it, the chance not only to
prove that Quebeckers accepted the package, but to establish the principle that sovereignty resides in the people of
Canada and not their governments.

In the aftermath of the 1982 constitutional patriation,
the myth took root both in Quebec nationalist enclaves and

in academic and political circles elsewhere in Canada that Quebec had been excluded from the Constitution. The myth, which drew sustenance from vivid accounts of "the night of the long knives," created a new climate of constitutional tension. It created also a submyth – that Quebec somehow had to be "brought back into the constitutional family." Not surprisingly, the myth was promoted by Quebec separatists, who continued to reject all federal efforts at constitutional reform. Unfortunately it was also promoted by the new Conservative government of Brian Mulroney. Elected in 1984, Mulroney's government enjoyed the support of many Quebec nationalists and numbered nationalists among its elected MPs, Lucien Bouchard and Gilles Loiselle, to name two. His harsh rhetoric about Quebec's "exclusion" from the Constitution may have been politically astute, vis-à-vis his Quebec nationalist base, but each of the constitutional initiatives it spawned failed, and the memory of it eventually came to haunt Canadians.

The reality is that Quebec has always been a part of the Constitution – legally and on the basis of Quebeckers' public support.

"IF CANADA IS TO BE A NATION AT ALL"

What has chafed Quebec's nationalists almost as much as the issue of language has been the alleged intrusion of the federal government into areas of provincial jurisdiction, especially social policy. Following the Second World War, Ottawa indeed staked a strong claim to social-policy jurisdiction, not only by means of constitutional amendments (for unemployment insurance and pensions) but also through the use of the so-called spending power to induce provinces to join various national programs. The result has been that Canadians have come to see their social programs – however much they may be in need of reform – as one of the country's most powerful unifying features.

The 1867 Constitution was fuzzy on allocating jurisdiction over social policy. This is hardly surprising since Confederation predated the modern welfare state. When the Canadian government took the first steps in the 1920s and 1930s toward shaping the welfare state, it collided with the "watertight compartments" constitutional vision held by Britain's Judicial Committee of the Privy Council. The law lords ruled that matters such as unemployment insurance fell within the exclusive provincial jurisdiction over property and civil rights. They also greatly limited federal authority under the Constitution's trade and commerce power and the general powers to legislate for peace, order, and good government. Thus, federal legislative initiatives to control prices and price-gouging (1919, 1922),* to set national labour standards (1935) in accordance with international treaty obligations, and to establish an unemployment insurance scheme were all found to be unconstitutional. Ways were sought to overcome these restrictive rulings, in particular to tackle the problem of how the provinces could financially shoulder the ever-growing constitutional responsibilities dumped on them by judicial decisions while,

---

* For example, in the 1922 *Board of Commerce* case, Lord Haldane held that a federal statute aimed at eliminating profiteering in the Ottawa retail clothing business in inflationary postwar conditions was not a valid application of the federal trade and commerce power (Section 91[2] of the Constitution Act, 1867), but the regulation of a particular trade which would come under provincial jurisdiction over property and civil rights.

constitutionally, the federal government had access to the
greater share of revenues.

The Royal Commission on Dominion–Provincial Relations (the Rowell–Sirois Commission) was established in
1937 to find a new constitutional equilibrium between
the distribution of federal and provincial powers and the
financial resources required by the two levels of government to meet their obligations. It recommended, in 1940, a
rational system of "national adjustment grants" – whereby
the federal government would make special grants to the
poorer provinces (the predecessor of equalization payments) – and it made a powerful case for national standards:

> In Canada today, freedom of movement and equality of
> opportunity are more important than ever before, and
> these depend in part on the maintenance of at least
> minimum national standards for education, public
> health and care of the indigent. . . . Not only national
> duty and decency, if Canada is to be a nation at all, but
> equity and national self-interest demand that the resi-
> dents of these [economically distressed] areas be given
> average services and equal opportunities. . . .

THE SPENDING POWER AND
SHARED-COST PROGRAMS

The national adjustment grants were rejected at the time by
the three wealthiest provinces (British Columbia, Alberta,
and Ontario, which would have received nothing under the
proposed system). There was, however, prompt federal–
provincial agreement to amend the Constitution to give
the Parliament of Canada legislative jurisdiction to create

national schemes for unemployment insurance (Section 91[2A]) and pensions (Section 94A).

With respect to many other social programs and expenditures, the federal government claimed authority to spend (known as "the spending power") in areas of exclusive provincial jurisdiction as long as it did not directly regulate them. This spending power was exercised in part, in the context of what are known as shared-cost programs, with Ottawa deciding upon the desirability of a particular program and then proposing it to the provinces on the basis of the federal and provincial governments each paying half the cost. Since the Second World War, at least one hundred shared-cost programs have been initiated by the federal government. For example, general medicare and hospital insurance – clearly within provincial jurisdiction and directly regulated by the provinces – were initiated by Ottawa by means of federal funds (so-called fifty-cent dollars) granted to the provinces on condition that the programs function in accord with federal stipulations or, more precisely, national standards. No province at the outset legally challenged the federal government's course, although complaints were soon voiced about how federal shared-cost programs would distort provincial spending priorities, by requiring certain levels of provincial expenditures to trigger the federal expenditure. Moreover, effectively, the provinces had no choice but to go along with the program. As constitutional scholar Peter Hogg points out, "refusal of the grant [the fifty-cent dollars] wears an aspect of taxation without benefit, since the residents of a non-participating province would still have to pay the federal taxes which finance the federal share of the programme in the other provinces."

In fact, Parliament's spending power has a firm constitutional base in that it can be clearly *inferred* from the federal powers to tax (Section 91[3]), to legislate with respect to "public property" (Section 91[1A]), and to appropriate federal funds (Section 106). According to a 1969 federal government discussion paper placed before the provinces during talks leading to the Victoria Charter, the justification for the spending power "is to be found in the very nature of the modern federal state – in the economic and technological interdependence, in the interdependence of the policies of its several governments, and in the sense of community which moves its residents to contribute to the well-being of residents in other parts of the federation."

In terms that presage those of the constitutional debate almost twenty years later, the discussion paper went on to provide examples of the interdependence that dictated federal action:

> The effectiveness of pollution control, for example, affects the people in neighbouring provinces; provincial educational systems contribute or fail to advance the economic growth of Canada as a whole; and the equality of opportunity across the country, or the lack of it, affects the well-being of Canadians generally. . . . Moreover, the mobility of Canadians – increasing year by year – itself creates a kind of interdependence: a person in almost any part of Canada, accustomed to the expectation that his children will sooner or later move to other parts of the country, develops an interest in the public services in other provinces as well as public services in his own province – hospital and medical care being the most obvious examples.

The discussion paper also put forward a proposal to limit the federal government's power to establish new national shared-cost programs in areas of provincial jurisdiction by requiring the federal government to first obtain "broad national consensus in favour of the programme." (Specifically the paper proposed the support of at least five provinces – at least two Western provinces and two Atlantic provinces – and support from three out of four of the senatorial districts: that is, Ontario, Quebec, the West, and Atlantic Canada). In addition, those provinces which chose to opt out of the program would be entitled to compensation, but the compensation would be paid to the *citizens* of the opted-out province, not to their provincial government. The fact that the provincial government would have to tax its residents in order to get access to the compensation provided a safeguard against a provincial government opting out without popular support.

Provincial criticism of the federal spending power, which Ottawa's opting-out-with-compensation proposal was intended to meet, generally focussed on conditional program grants and subsidies to provinces for the reasons stated above. (Unconditional payments – especially direct federal payments to individuals, the most prominent examples being family allowances and old age security – were not particularly problematic.)

While the 1969 proposal was never formally implemented, over subsequent years Ottawa responded to provincial criticisms by significantly relaxing the shared-cost rules in several ways. It changed its contributions to "established programs" such as post-secondary education, medicare, and hospital insurance from cash-only to a combination of cash and conceded tax points to the provinces (thus weakening its leverage over provincial behaviour). And with the 1977 Established Programs Financing (EPF) Act, it also abandoned the sharing of actual provincial operating costs in favour of a formula which calculates the federal contribution according to the growth of the economy and the growth of provincial populations. (Under the new 1977 EPF Act, the federal government offered the provinces combined cash and tax points equal in value to federal per-capita program contributions in the base year of 1975–76. The "block" transfers would then be escalated each year according to a moving average of GNP growth over the most recent three-year period. For its own budgetary purpose, Ottawa split the total transfer into 32 per cent for post-secondary education and 68 per cent for health.)

Ottawa preferred this shift from shared-cost funding to formula-driven block funding because it could control the transfers more easily. As much as the provinces had felt that 50-cent dollars distorted their spending priorities, so the federal government came to feel vulnerable to sudden increases in expenditure by the *provinces*.

Federal transfers under the other major shared-cost program which emerged in the 1960s (the Canada Assistance Plan for welfare costs), although conditional, were not particularly controversial until Ottawa unilaterally initiated cutbacks beginning in the late 1980s and ultimately abolished CAP in 1996. Indeed, provinces resisted a federal attempt in the 1970s to block-fund CAP. Shared-cost funding at least meant that in hard times, when the number of people on welfare increased, the federal contribution would have to increase in tandem. In any event, CAP transfers were subject to very minor federal conditions, notably an obligation by provinces not to refuse welfare assistance to those

in need on the basis of the recipient's province of origin and
to establish a procedure for appealing administrative welfare
decisions. And, in the face of the Quebec government's
insistence that its social services not be subject to national
standards, Ottawa agreed to special administrative arrangements with the province that allowed it to opt out completely and receive equivalent tax-point concessions in lieu
of cash transfers.

The few complaints that were heard about direct federal
transfers for family allowances ceased after arrangements
were made in 1974 to allow for provincial variation on how
the transfers were used. Quebec immediately took advantage of this to provide an incentive to families to have
more children. Alberta provided for another variation. The
provinces also appeared content when national maternity
benefits were shoehorned into the unemployment insurance program. It was an odd legislative home for them, but
UI provided the federal government with the necessary
jurisdictional base from which to act.

Federal transfers for medical care and hospital insurance,
however, have always been both highly conditional and
a source of federal–provincial friction. Tension reached a
peak in 1984 with passage of the Canada Health Act enshrining the principles – the conditions of federal transfers to the
provinces – of accessibility, universality, transferability
(portability), comprehensiveness, and public administration, as well as imposing federal penalties for hospital user
fees and doctors' extra billing.

Despite provincial protests, public support for the federal
role in health care has never been less than strong. Canadians
have made clear they do not want patchwork health care,
and patchwork health. Thus even as the current Liberal

government has moved out of an active, national social-policy role, has abolished the CAP and rolled all transfers into an effectively unconditional block transfer called the Canada Health and Social Transfer (CHST), it has insisted, to date, on enforcing the Canada Health Act to the fullest extent possible.

FEDERAL JURISDICTION IN
SOCIAL POLICY IS STRENGTHENED

The 1982 constitutional reforms and several judicial decisions since 1982 have strengthened federal jurisdiction in this vital area of national life. Section 36 of the Constitution Act, 1982, although it creates no new federal (or provincial) powers, provides a clear legitimacy for the federal government's spending power in social programs, at least for the purposes of assuring equity among individual Canadians. The section constitutionally *commits* Parliament and the provincial legislatures, together with the governments of Canada and the provinces to "promoting equal opportunities for the well-being of Canadians." It *commits* them to "furthering economic development to reduce disparity in opportunities." And it *commits* them to "providing essential public services of reasonable quality to all Canadians." What could be more unambiguous? It also *commits* Parliament and the government of Canada to "the principle of equalization payments to ensure that provincial governments have sufficient revenues to provide reasonably comparable levels of public services at reasonably comparable levels of taxation." Again, there is no ambiguity.

In the late 1980s and early 1990s, the Supreme Court of Canada for the first time explicitly acknowledged the use of the spending power as a constitutionally legitimate federal activity in areas of primary provincial jurisdiction.

The Court in this same period also reviewed what is known to constitutional scholars as "the national concern branch [or national dimensions branch]" of the POGG power, which had been reduced virtually to non-existence in the first half of the century by the Judicial Committee of the Privy Council. The "national concern branch" takes its name from a Judicial Committee dictum set down in the 1946 *Canada Temperance Foundation* case – with its history dating back to *Russell v. The Queen* (1882). Their Lordships laid down the concept that some matters wholly within provincial jurisdiction could become of such importance as to acquire national dimensions or national concern, and hence fall within Parliament's jurisdiction under the power to legislate for peace, order, and good government. As we have seen, however, under the Judicial Committee's narrow and at times contradictory interpretations, the national-interest branch was reduced to a shadow, something to be exercised only in an emergency, or in Lord Haldane's three infamous instances of famine, pestilence, and war. In 1946, however, Viscount Simon headed off in another direction by formulating a new test:

> In their Lordships' opinion, the true test must be found in the real subject matter of the legislation: if it is such that it goes beyond local or provincial concern or interests and must from its inherent nature be the concern of the Dominion as a whole (as, for example, in the *Aeronautics* case and the *Radio* case) then it will fall within the competence of the Dominion Parliament as a matter affecting the peace, order and

good government of Canada, although it may in
another aspect touch on matters specially reserved
to the provincial legislature. War and pestilence, no
doubt, are instances; so, too, may be the drink or drug
traffic, or the carrying of arms.

After 1949, when appeals to the Privy Council were
abolished and the Supreme Court of Canada became the
Constitution's final arbiter, the national-concern test came
to rest broadly on whether a subject of legislation had
nationwide importance, "of import or significance to all
parts of Canada," and met the qualifications of "singleness,
distinctiveness and indivisibility." Then, in the 1988 *Crown
Zellerbach* case (an environmental matter), the Supreme
Court took another step forward. In a 4–3 decision, it ruled
that Parliament could act in the national interest if an issue
otherwise falling within provincial jurisdiction was of
national concern and if the province was unable or unlikely
to act to serve the national interest. However, in exercising
the POGG power, the federal Parliament could impair
provincial jurisdiction only to the minimum extent necessary to fill the gap left by provincial inaction.

The Supreme Court made two other important decisions.
It revived the long-dormant federal trade and commerce
power to uphold the constitutionality of provisions of
federal competition law.[*] It also held that excessive legal
variation between provinces, even in areas of exclusive provincial jurisdiction, could impose substantial costs on the
federation as a whole, and in particular could impede or

---

[*] *General Motors of Canada v. City National Leasing* (1989)

distort economic and even personal mobility within Canada.*
These decisions opened the possibility of more vigorous
federal activity in establishing "national standards" and
"national frameworks" in a wide field of policy areas.

Finally, the Supreme Court affirmed exclusive provincial
jurisdiction over the delivery of health care. But it also left
some jurisdictional room for the federal government to be
involved in the setting of norms, goals, and ends with respect
to health care, possibly under the national-concern branch
of POGG, quite apart from the exercise of the spending
power.† This should be kept in mind as federal cash transfers for health care diminish to almost nothing in the
twenty-first century, and the federal government requires
an alternative source of leverage over the provinces.

What we see here is that the general constitutional and
policy context is now favourable to a broad rather than a
narrow reading of federal scope for involvement in social
policy. The Supreme Court has moved away from a narrow
or rigid view of federal power, recognizing the interconnec-
tion between national and local aspects of areas of policy
making such as environment or telecommunications, and
the importance of the federal general powers, both POGG
and trade and commerce. The federal government has been
assured sufficient scope to promote the national interest in
an era of global interdependence, particularly in the area of
social policy.

Social policy is viewed in many countries in today's era of
globalization as being closely linked with economic policy

---

* *Hunt v. Workers' Compensation Board et al.* (1993)
† *R. v. Morgentaler* (1993), following *R. v. Schneider* (1982)

generally, and with trade policy more specifically. Social
clauses in trade agreements in NAFTA, and the making of
transnational social policy – relating, for example, to some
social standards in the European Union – make it clear that
such matters cannot be left exclusively to lower levels of
government, or indeed to any one level of government.

Economic change, whether cyclical (such as a recession)
or structural, affects different regions in different degrees at
different times. Sharing the burden of these changes means
a national role not only in adjustment policy, but in the full
range of policies that provide a safety net for individuals
hard hit by change, including welfare, unemployment benefits, retraining and relocation assistance, health care, social
work, and counselling.

AND YET THE FEDERAL GOVERNMENT
WITHDRAWS
Just at a time when the courts, economic and social pres-
sures, and concerns over equity all point to a more vigorous
role for the federal government in setting national standards, the federal government appears intent on diminishing its capacity.

Admittedly, federal transfers are still substantial. Prior to
winding up the Canada Assistance Plan (CAP) in 1995, federal
transfers to provinces amounted to about $40 billion, of
which $22 billion was paid for Established Program Finan-
cing (EPF), $7.8 billion under CAP, and $7.9 billion in equalization payments. Nevertheless, all signs point to significant
ongoing reductions in federal transfers and correspond-
ingly reduced federal policy leverage in the future. Leverage
depends on the transfer of actual cash rather than tax

points, and the cash transfer is due to disappear early in the twenty-first century. The basis for a federal role in setting national standards will have to rest either (questionably) on leveraging unrelated cash transfers, or in finding alternative jurisdictional grounds in POGG, the trade and commerce power, and the like.

In winding up CAP and creating the Canada Health and Social Transfer (CHST), the federal government appears to have abandoned national standards in respect of social assistance and social services. The stated objective for removing national standards for social assistance and social services is to give the provinces more flexibility. But at what cost for national equity?

There are now incentives for provinces to cut welfare entitlements so as not to attract the poor from other provinces. And, with British Columbia's enactment of residency requirements for social assistance, there may well be a patchwork of eligibility requirements emerging across the country depending on the outcome of the ongoing federal–provincial "social union" discussions.[*] Finally, it is highly probable that, in these days of tight money, provinces will allocate by far the most money to health and education rather than to welfare.

It is a vain hope that the provinces will co-operate among themselves and formulate interprovincial "national

---

[*] For the moment, the federal government was able to prevent the British Columbia action in a negotiated agreement dated March 6, 1997, as follows: "The Prime Minister and the Premier agreed that a national multilateral process, with all parties consulted on its design, would advance everyone's interest in protecting and promoting mobility in Canada. The Government of Canada will raise the issue with all the provinces and work toward a national solution in two years."

standards." This is at best naïve, at worst an abandonment of federal constitutional responsibilities under Section 36 – which was certainly the warning a parliamentary committee heard during public hearings as part of the review of the social security system in 1994–95. If anything, there was a public call for strengthening the national standards under CAP, not discarding them. Yet such is the worry in Ottawa about offending provincial government sensibilities, known as the Charlottetown mindset of Mulroney-era federal bureaucrats, that it may be impossible to reverse the inexorable shrinking of federal roles and responsibilities.

With the federal government in retreat, the provinces took the initiative. A December 1995 report of the provincial Ministerial Council on Social Policy Reform and Renewal (in which all provinces except Quebec participated) suggested that income support for children could be consolidated into a single *national* program, jointly managed by the federal government and the provinces. The report also recommended a *national* income security program for persons with disabilities. In addition, it promoted the idea of an integrated support program for working-age adults without disabilities that would merge provincial social assistance and federal Employment Insurance programs and could involve elements of both federal and provincial delivery. What is meant by joint management of integrated programs is left unclear, but at least the endorsement of national approaches to social policy was a good sign. Ironically, these recommendations closely resemble those put forward at the 1945 Dominion–Provincial Conference on Reconstruction more than fifty years ago.

However, the provinces' stated openness to new national programs was offset by their proposal that "federal activity in areas of sole provincial responsibility should occur only after federal/provincial/territorial agreement on how federal spending can be effectively applied." If this provision were put into effect, the ability of the federal government to use its spending power in the national interest would be fettered perhaps even more than was proposed in the aborted Meech Lake and Charlottetown accords, since each province or territory would have a veto over any proposal for a national program.

In addition, the report implied that "national standards" could be developed and implemented by the provinces acting alone, without the help of the federal government. As social policy expert Michael Mendelson noted in a Caledon Institute of Social Policy commentary (June 1996): "The track record on interprovincial agreements is very poor. About the only meaningful agreement anyone can point to in the last 50 years is the recent deal on interprovincial trade."

It is doubtful that the provinces will agree to standards with any meaning or substance. Will British Columbia, for example, agree *not* to reimpose a provincial residency requirement for social assistance? Moreover, even if provinces did agree to substantive standards, they could not be enforced. If one province broke the standard, the standard would simply cease to be a national standard. At least with the interprovincial trade agreement, one province can retaliate against another, as Ontario did in respect of Quebec's construction practices.

In response to the provinces' 1995 Ministerial Council report, the federal government has pursued a collaborative approach with the provinces regarding what is increasingly known as the social union. The 1996 Speech from the Throne committed the federal government to essentially neutering

the spending power. Henceforth, it will not use the spending power to create new shared-cost programs in areas of
exclusive provincial jurisdiction without the consent of a
majority of provinces, and it will compensate any non-
participating province if the province undertakes equivalent or comparable initiatives. (This is the rejected Meech/
Charlottetown proposal discussed later.) This marked the
official end to any federal child-care proposal.

The unemployment insurance reforms legislated in
recent years provided for a significant transfer of responsibility for labour-market programs to the provinces.[*] The
agreements with the provinces, however, must proscribe
provincially set minimum periods of residence, and the
federal government retained responsibility for a national
labour-market information and exchange system to support
interprovincial mobility of labour.

At the June 1996 first ministers' meeting, all governments
agreed to pursue the concept of a National Child Benefit
system, and the 1997 federal budget proposed to increase
the more than $5.1 billion currently spent on the existing
Child Tax Benefit, to a $6.6 billion commitment, starting
in July 1998. Provinces could reduce their social assistance

---

[*] By the 1997 election, the federal government had, in fact, concluded
bilateral labour market agreements with eight provinces (excluding
Ontario and Saskatchewan) of which four involved significant devolution,
including substantial transfers of money from the federal government to
the provinces, and the transfer of some 1,600 federal officials to provincial employment. The director of the Institute of Intergovernmental
Relations at Queen's University, Harvey Lazar, notes ironically regarding
the labour market agreements: "To the extent there may have been significant duplication of federal and provincial activity, which was never
demonstrated and almost certainly did not exist, it will be reduced."

payments on behalf of children by the amount of the increase in the federal child benefit, and reinvest the savings into programs to improve work incentives, benefits, and services for low-income families with children.

The ongoing federal–provincial discussions may also be expanded to address a wider National Children's Agenda – involving federal and provincial Health and Justice ministries as well. At the same time, since 1996, federal–provincial discussions on Disability Income and Supports have been pursuing more federal–provincial coherence in helping Canadians with disabilities. This, however, is made difficult by the need to co-ordinate the two earnings-replacement programs – Workers' Compensation (solely provincial) and the Canada Pension Plan, involving different financing arrangements on the part of employers and employees.

Finally, in August 1997, the provincial premiers "expressed their desire to strengthen the role of the Federal/Provincial/Territorial Council on Social Policy Renewal in co-ordinating and monitoring ... work on social policy renewal." They then proposed adding to the already wide and complex agenda.

It remains to be seen where all this "collaboration" will lead – to a strengthened "social union" with a strong, creative federal government playing a leading role, or to incoherent, counter-productive policy responses in which the federal government continues to hide behind provincial governments. As of going to press, a first ministers conference that was to have constructed a framework of principles for the Canadian social union was cancelled. Among other things, an impasse was developing over provincial proposals that would block Ottawa from unilaterally establishing even non-shared-cost programs such as the Millennium Scholarship Fund (a bursary program for college and university students), or national systems of drug insurance or home care.

CODA

Although the foregoing discussion has focussed on social programs, it is important to note that many federal shared-cost programs established through the "spending power" were in areas outside social policy, notably regional economic development. For example, the General Development Agreements (GDAs) of the 1970s, and then the umbrella Economic and Regional Development Agreements (ERDAs) in the 1980s, were highly conditional, and tied to specific projects or to the creation of specific assistance programs. In the case of ERDAs in particular, emphasis was placed on co-ordinated planning, with parallel service delivery by the federal and provincial governments. Federal fiscal constraints have now led to the gradual elimination of many of these programs during the 1990s.

CHAPTER 6

THE MORASS OF MEECH

Four years ago, Canada was a peaceable and a fairly happy kingdom. . . . Throughout Canada there was little interest in further constitutional reform. Only a handful of academics and politicians still rooted through the entrails of our past struggles. Then, at Meech Lake, the first ministers naively opened up the Constitution, literally conspired to ram through fundamental changes to our country with no regard to what the people thought and tried to scare dissenters by threatening national collapse if their accord failed. When failure came, one year ago this month, Mulroney, Peterson, Bourassa and Co. had legitimized the idea of Canada's disintegration. It has been with us ever since. In four short years, a "status quo" that generated peace, order, good government and prosperity for the better part of 120 years had become intolerable.

— Historian Michael Bliss, *The Globe and Mail*, June 14, 1991

THE MEECH LAKE ACCORD has been likened by former Ontario premier David Peterson (who signed it) to the execution of Louis Riel in its cleaving of Quebec and the rest of Canada. This is a fey reading of history. The execution of Riel had significant public support on one half of Canada's language divide. Meech Lake didn't. Its rejection was almost as marked in French-speaking Canada as it was in English-speaking Canada. Far from a noble mission to save the country that foundered on the rocks of "intolerance" (David Peterson's word), Meech Lake was both an authoritarian attempt by governments to change the country's fundamental law in the face of massive public opposition and a crafty plan by some Quebec nationalists to slip the province out of Confederation through a back door.

The story begins in 1984 with the election of Brian Mulroney's Conservatives with the help of Quebec nationalists, a number of whom were given key positions in the cabinet. They included Gilles Loiselle, the *péquiste* agent general in London, and Monique Vézina, who in a later television interview admitted she had never been a federalist, even while a member of the Mulroney government. At his nomination meeting in Sept-Iles, Mulroney had vowed that, if he became prime minister, he would make it possible for Quebec to accept the Constitution "with honour and enthusiasm." In the minds of the country's, and Quebec's, dominant political and academic elites, the time seemed propitious for constitutional change.

A year later, in 1985, Robert Bourassa's nominally federalist Liberal party was returned to power in Quebec. Bourassa almost immediately presented a set of five "minimum" conditions or demands that would, it was said, permit Quebec's government and National Assembly to accept the 1982 constitutional amendments. The five conditions were:

- that the Constitution, in its preamble, would explicitly recognize Quebec as a "distinct society";
- that Quebec would be given a veto over constitutional change;

- that Quebec would have a role in the appointment of Supreme Court judges;
- that restrictions would be placed on the federal spending power;
- that Quebec would be given increased power over immigration.

In his response to Bourassa's demands, Mulroney took the position that Meech was to be the "Quebec Round" of constitutional negotiations, since Quebec had been "forgotten" in 1982. Accordingly, he was prepared to accept all of Bourassa's demands and, indeed, to extend them to other provinces to secure unanimous agreement, an approach that succeeded spectacularly in June 1987, when the Prime Minister and the provincial premiers gathered at the government conference facility at Meech Lake across the river from Ottawa in Quebec's Gatineau Hills.

Mulroney's leading constitutional adviser was Lucien Bouchard – subsequently leader of the separatist Bloc Québécois and Parti Québécois premier of Quebec – who helped draft Mulroney's speeches on "national reconciliation." In his autobiography, he described his strategy for the Meech Lake process:

> I supported a policy of national reconciliation in order eventually to espouse *le beau risque*. The ultimate objective was to fundamentally redo the division of powers for the benefit of Quebec. . . . I imagined that the ratification of Meech would create a spirit of openness towards the historic demands of Quebec. One could hope that . . . Quebec would be able to put on

the table a proposal for fundamental restructuring
of the Canadian constitution.

In other words, for Bouchard (and many Quebec nationalists), Meech Lake was seen from the outset as a first step
in a long process of constitutional reform which would
lead to sovereignty-association, while at the same time
correct the alleged isolation and humiliation suffered by
Quebec in 1982.

The accord conceded more to so-called provincial
rights than had been given up by any federal government
since Confederation. Quebec was given its "distinct society"
recognition. The power of all provinces over immigration
was increased; judges of the Supreme Court were to be
appointed from lists of candidates submitted by all the
provinces; all the provinces were to be given the right to
opt out from federal–provincial shared-cost programs, with
compensation, provided they undertook their own programs compatible with national "objectives"; the existing
constitutional amending formula was left untouched but the
unanimity rule was expanded so that each province could
exercise a veto over changes to the Senate and the Supreme
Court and admission to Confederation of new provinces.

The "distinct society" condition was no more, no less,
than the perennial demand by Quebec's provincial political
elites for "special status" within the federal structure. The
expanded constitutional powers flowing from this "special
status" were claimed as necessary to ensure Quebec's long-
term cultural and linguistic security, and to increase
Quebec's powers vis-à-vis the federal government in the
preservation and promotion of Quebec's French collectivity. Before Meech, no federal government or prime minister

had been willing to cede this special role to Quebec. Instead, the federal government and Parliament – while respecting provincial constitutional powers – had played a mainly consistent role in protecting and promoting both the franco-phone majority and anglophone minorities in Quebec and the francophone minority outside Quebec, and in promoting, in general, official bilingualism across Canada.

Those who had long opposed special status for Quebec were alive to its dangers: that it would be simply a step on the road to Quebec independence; that granting the Quebec government extra constitutional powers not enjoyed by other provinces would mean Quebec MPs in Ottawa could no longer vote on national matters which, in Quebec, would now fall within provincial jurisdiction (or, if they could, they would be voting on matters which would not apply in Quebec); that gradually Quebeckers would come to see themselves in the mirror of Ottawa politics as a second-class, peripheral people and look more and more to their provincial government for state activity (which is what is now happening, with the federal government's withdrawal from social policy). Separation under "special status" or "distinct society" would be a quieter, more gradual process than the dramatic outcome of a Yes vote in an independence referendum, but it would be no less final.

We examine the substance of the Meech Lake Accord in detail.

DISTINCT SOCIETY CLAUSE
The Meech Lake Accord elevated Quebec's demand for recognition as a distinct society into a constitutional inter-pretative clause – meaning a clause determining how the

whole Constitution would be "read" and applied. The Quebec "government and legislature" were given a special role to "preserve and promote" the province's distinct society and distinct identity, a mandate which could positively permit the Quebec government to infringe upon the protections of the Charter of Rights and Freedoms in order to further the collective interests of the French-speaking majority.

To understand clearly how this would work, consider the 1988 case in which the Supreme Court of Canada declared that Quebec legislation decreeing that only French could be used on commercial signs was an unjustifiable infringement on freedom of expression. To circumvent the Court's ruling, the Quebec government invoked the Charter's so-called notwithstanding, or override, clause. This clause, Section 33, says Parliament or a provincial legislature may "expressly declare" that a law shall operate *notwithstanding* its conflict with certain specified rights and freedoms which the Charter otherwise protects. Many legal experts – along with the late Premier Bourassa himself – have pointed out that, had the distinct society clause been a part of the Constitution in 1988, there would have been no need for the Quebec government to invoke Section 33. It would have been enough simply, and effortlessly and without fear of judicial scrutiny, to cite Section 1, which states that the Charter's rights and freedoms are subject to such limits as can be "demonstrably justified" in a democratic society (with the distinct society clause providing the necessary justification).

Some attempt at the Meech Lake conference was made to "Canadianize" the clause with simultaneous recognition of

Canada's French-speaking and English-speaking character as a "fundamental characteristic" of Canada. Yet the role for other governments was merely to "preserve," not "preserve and promote," those characteristics, wording that unquestionably confirmed the asymmetry of the obligations. The preserve-only obligation also implied a freezing of the status of French-speaking minorities outside Quebec who faced provincial governments less than sympathetic to their language and educational rights – and, indeed, even "freezing" was an overstatement. In 1988, the governments of Saskatchewan and Alberta coldly trampled on the spirit of the Meech Lake Accord, which they had signed just a year earlier, by using a complicated bit of constitutional mechanics to strip their official minorities of language rights in provincial courts and legislatures.

The Supreme Court ruled in 1988 that Saskatchewan was obligated to translate all its laws into French as required by an 1877 amendment to the North-West Territories Act giving equal status to French and English in the legislative council and in proceedings before the courts. In 1891, however, the territorial legislature was empowered by Parliament to "regulate its proceedings" and it promptly discarded the official use of French. Alberta, Saskatchewan, and Manitoba were carved out of the North-West Territories, and the legislation creating them provided that laws in force in the territories would generally continue in the new provinces.

However, while language guarantees were expressly stated in the statute creating Manitoba as a province, and thus were deemed by the Supreme Court, in 1985, to be constitutionally entrenched, they were not in the 1905 legislation creating Alberta and Saskatchewan as provinces, despite an eloquent appeal for their inclusion by Henri Bourassa. Thus the Supreme Court ruled that Saskatchewan (and, by extension, Alberta) had a choice: it could either comply with the language-rights provision of the North-West Territories Act – and translate, re-enact, and print all statutes in French – or, alternatively, it could enact a new statute repealing the language-rights provision and declare all existing provincial statutes valid even though they had been enacted and printed solely in English. Saskatchewan chose the latter course over the objections of its franco-phone minority.

Alberta promptly followed Saskatchewan's lead, offering its minority even fewer concessions than its sister province, which had permitted French to be spoken in the legislature and courts, though official records would be in English only, and had proposed that some "key statutes" might be translated. Alberta offered no translation of statutes. It offered the right to speak in the legislature in French only with the permission of the Speaker and the right to use French (with interpreters) in court proceedings.

In vain, Mulroney appealed to the governments of Alberta and Saskatchewan for a higher national purpose – as ninety years earlier Laurier had made his "sunny ways" appeal to the Manitoba government not to eradicate support for separate schools. But the *coup de grâce* in the West was delivered by the Quebec government itself, which, with a cold eye on the rights of its anglophone minority, intervened before the Supreme Court *against* francophone Albertans seeking minority control of their own schools under Section 23 of the Charter. The two-nation theory was again rearing its ugly head.

In the Meech Lake deal-making, there was a last-minute

insertion of words that said that nothing in the distinct society clause would affect Charter provisions dealing with aboriginal rights and Canada's multicultural heritage. Those words served only to increase the level of concern over what the distinct society clause actually meant, because, by negative inference, they exposed all other Charter rights to the impact of the distinct society clause. That is, if aboriginal and multicultural rights were not affected by the distinct society clause, then everything else must be.

The distinct society clause clearly took the Constitution *away from* the 1982 amendments which emphasized individual linguistic rights in an officially bilingual Canada and *toward* the notion of a territorial- and state-based dualism – French in Quebec, English outside Quebec. Thus, in general, the distinct society clause undermined the idea that all Canadians have common rights and freedoms regardless of where they live. It did this by directing that the entire Constitution, including the Charter, be interpreted in light of geographic and sociocultural considerations. In other words, the nature of basic rights would henceforth vary, depending on which province Canadians lived in, which linguistic group they belonged to, and so forth.

The clause could also affect interpretation of the division of powers in the so-called grey areas of the Constitution that were not foreseen in 1867 when federal and provincial spheres of jurisdiction were originally established. Communications, for example. Armed with the distinct society clause, the Quebec government could now argue that it was entitled to special powers in order to discharge special responsibility toward the French-speaking majority.

CONSTITUTIONAL AMENDMENT
– AND THE VETO

The Meech Lake Accord gave all provinces the same veto over an enlarged number of constitutional amendments, including the creation of new provinces and reform of the Senate. Where would this lead? Had the accord been ratified by Parliament and all provincial legislatures, it would have led to a straitjacket, and to the Constitution being removed even further from the sovereign control of the Canadian people by enhancing the amending authority of governments. It would have made the Constitution's most appropriate preamble not "We, the people of Canada . . .," not even "We, the people of Ontario, Quebec, British Columbia . . .," but rather "We, the premiers of Ontario, Quebec, British Columbia. . . ."

The Meech Lake signatories, to further satisfy Quebec's demands, altered the 1982 *general* amending formula (requiring agreement of seven provinces having 50 per cent of the population) to provide that, for any amendments affecting the division of powers, reasonable compensation would be paid to any province which chose not to agree. This was full acceptance of the so-called Gang of Eight provincial consensus of 1981, and was the crowning victory of the provincialist thrust to anatomize Canada. With this formula in place, provincial leverage over national policy making would have been greatly increased. If ever again there was to be an attempt to amend the Constitution to strengthen federal jurisdiction for the national purpose – as had been required for unemployment insurance and old-age pensions and could be required again, say, for the economic union, securities regulation, or the environment – what incentive would there be for the provinces to take part? They could just painlessly opt out, with the obvious implication that no such amendment would ever take place. When, as under the existing amending formula, there is no constitutionalized compensation for opting out, up to three dissenting provinces have an incentive to bargain and to seek an acceptable compromise so that they do not lose their share of national expenditures.

THE APPOINTMENT OF JUDGES

The Meech Lake Accord offered all provinces a significant role in nominating justices of the Supreme Court of Canada, something that went far beyond Quebec's request for consultation on appointments. Under the existing system, the prime minister makes the appointments following reasonably extensive consultation with the legal community among others. Under the accord, the federal government would have been required to make judicial appointments from lists prepared by the provincial governments which inevitably would have produced an obvious provincializing influence on the Court. Overall, this provision took the appointment process in the direction opposite to that favoured in large part by the legal profession and the people. Instead of a transparent and open system in keeping with the more politically charged role played by the Court in interpreting the Charter of Rights and Freedoms, the proposed process would have been more closed and inaccessible.

We have already noted the enormous influence the Judicial Committee of the Privy Council had on Canada's constitutional development up to 1949. Had the Supreme Court of Canada become predominantly provincialist in outlook, as the Meech Lake Accord invited it to become, one could have expected a similar bias in its decisions, leading to a steady erosion of federal power and authority.

THE SPENDING POWER

The accord significantly limited the federal government's use of its spending power to establish national programs in areas of exclusive provincial jurisdiction. It permitted provinces to opt out of national programs, with compensation, so long as they established programs of their own which met the "objectives" of the national scheme. This effectively precluded the establishment of minimum national standards ("objectives" are not "standards"). It also handed the provinces a massive disincentive to join with the federal government in pursuing important national social-policy and equity-adjustment goals. National public opinion would hardly have supported a project whereby the federal government raised revenues to finance a program, only to turn the money over to provincial governments as some sort of anonymous benefactor.

And who would have had to decide whether an opting-out province qualified for compensation? Meech would have placed on the courts the whole burden of scrutinizing and weighing matters of public policy, and determining whether provincial programs met the "objectives" of given national programs.

Supporters of limitations on the spending power – apart from those who oppose it on the ideological grounds of provincial supremacy – have argued that in times of fiscal restraint profligate federal governments need a brake on the exchequer. They claim that federal spending in areas of provincial jurisdiction is a (politically) logical place to cut, and cut deeply. But the spending power is not simply a matter of spending money. It is a mechanism by which the federal government pursues national policy objectives, and it is important to ensure that the federal government can, in the future, establish and enforce national standards in a wide range of policy areas – for example: a national child-care program, a comprehensive disability insurance scheme, a national science and technology strategy, environmental protection, a national commitment to improving the quality and accessibility of education at all levels, the integration of our social assistance and employment policies, and new services to cope with our ageing population. Spending better and more wisely is always a laudable goal.

POWERS OVER IMMIGRATION

The accord provided for bilateral agreements between Ottawa and any province "relating to immigration or the temporary admission of aliens into that province that is appropriate to the needs and circumstances of that province." These agreements could be entrenched in the Constitution and changed only by using the constitutional amending procedure or (if fewer than seven provinces concluded agreements) by "such other manner as is set out in the [specific provincial] agreement."

In addition, the accord allowed every province to receive 5 per cent more immigrants than was warranted by its demographic weight within the federation. This was another classic illustration of a federal concession to Quebec being "generalized" to the other provinces so as to bring them onside. The 5 per cent "bonus" was intended to offset Quebec's concern over its relative population decline. It was completely unrealistic. Immigrants once landed are free to go anywhere in Canada, and, indeed, Quebec immigrants and native anglophone Quebeckers have chosen and continue to choose to leave the province. As for the accord's provision granting every province 5 per cent more immigrants than their proportional share, it was simply a mathematical impossibility. (Altogether, the provinces would have been entitled to 150 per cent of the pool of immigrants.) As the great constitutional expert Eugene Forsey put it, with this proposal "the whole immigration system could be shredded." No longer would there be a coherent national immigration program, an essential element of any nation's policy apparatus. Instead there potentially would be ten different immigration policies, with immigrants being "integrated" not into Canada but into a province. Such a provincialization of immigration could only marginally have been offset by the federal government's ability to set "national standards and objectives" (which include establishing "general classes of immigrants" – i.e., family, independent, entrepreneurial – and setting the total number of immigrants).

WAIT, THERE'S MORE
Finally, Mulroney threw in a couple of provisions that were never part of Quebec's list. All provinces were to be allowed to put forward names for senators from which the federal government would be required to select new appointments to the Upper House, and annual first ministers' conferences (both on constitutional reform and on the economy and other matters) were to be constitutionally entrenched. Together, these two provisions were a provincialist triumph.

The provinces would now control the composition of two important federal institutions – the Senate and the Supreme Court. And a new edifice of superior government for the country's governance – the First Ministers' Conference – was invested with concrete purpose and given constitutional status. No longer was there to be a clear voice speaking for "Canada," only the disparate chorus of self-interested provincial politicians. The federal government was to become simply an agent of the provinces. The dreams of Honoré Mercier, Oliver Mowat and their like were to be fulfilled. The compact theory of Confederation was to be victorious. The Fathers of Confederation were to be left spinning in their graves.

Mulroney's Senate proposal fell on stony ground. Those provinces zealously interested in major reform of the Upper House, particularly those favouring a so-called Triple-E Senate (Elected members, Equal representation from all provinces, and Effective powers vis-à-vis the House of Commons) realized that if they accepted the Prime Minister's offer of provincial influence over the composition of the Senate *in its existing form*, further changes would likely be impossible. (Meech Lake's amending formula extended the unanimity rule to the Senate, and Ontario and Quebec with their huge numbers of Commons seats would have no reason to want an "effective" Senate in which their representation was "equal" to that of smaller provinces.) This was one of many illustrations of the ineptitude of Meech Lake's drafters and the dangers of proceeding without public consultation.

WHAT WENT WRONG:
PROCESS, PROCESS, PROCESS

The accord failed as much because of the elitist, secretive process that produced it as because of its substance. What Mulroney and the premiers inadequately appreciated – or chose not to appreciate – was that the 1982 constitutional reforms which they all so denigrated flowed from genuine public consultations. The joint Senate–Commons committee that considered the reforms was the first committee in Parliament's history to have its proceedings televised. It sat for 267 hours over 56 days through the fall and winter of 1980–81. It heard from 914 individuals and 294 groups and spent more than 90 hours on a clause-by-clause examination of the Charter, earning its 25 members the affectionately good-humoured label "the Fathers of Reconfederation."

No such amiable, public dynamic touched Meech, the cold, covert fiat of eleven white men in suits.

Although brief hearings on the Meech Accord were held in Quebec, Ontario, and the national capital, they were after-the-fact forums devoid of meaning. Opponents – which included all those "Charter Canadians" (in the label of political scientist Alan Cairns) who rightly saw themselves as having been excluded from the accord and the process. Women's groups, aboriginal groups, multicultural communities, and other social clusters who had become attached to the 1982 "people's" Constitution, as well as Northerners whom Meech Lake all but disenfranchised, were told simply that the accord could not be reopened, and that any additional constitutional modifications would have to await further first ministers' discussions. For the Meech Accord to move from clubby first ministers' agreement to constitutional law, however, it had to be ratified by each provincial legislature and both Houses of Parliament within three years of the first ratification. The dismissive attitude of the accord's architects strengthened the determination of the accord's opponents to block that ratification.

It is difficult to overemphasize the gulf between public and the elites that the Meech Accord controversy revealed. It is perhaps equally difficult to understand how politicians could come to be so at odds with the people to whom they were democratically accountable and dependent upon for re-election. In his book, *Fathoming Meech Lake*, constitutional scholar Bryan Schwartz writes:

> Those who believe in responsible government and participatory democracy have every reason to be outraged by the autocratic approach to constitutional reform adopted by first ministers. It is an affront to cabinet democracy for first ministers to agree to anything as significant as constitutional reform without consulting their cabinets. It is demeaning to the role of the legislature for elected members to have no opportunity to debate the merits of an accord until after the first minister has presented them with a fait accompli. It is contemptuous of the right of the people to be consulted for most first ministers to eschew public hearings, for all but the Premier of Quebec to postpone public input until after the formulation of a practically final draft.

The wheels of the accord started loosening within months of it being signed. New Brunswick elected a Liberal government led by Frank McKenna, who was unable to accept the accord's impact on the Charter of Rights. Manitoba elected a minority Conservative government led by Gary Filmon; the province's opposition Liberals and New Democrats both opposed the accord. On December 19, 1988, the day after the Quebec government used the Constitution's notwithstanding clause to override the Supreme Court of Canada's decision on the province's language law for signs, Manitoba premier Gary Filmon withdrew the resolution from before the provincial legislature to ratify the accord. Newfoundland elected a Liberal government led by Clyde Wells, a formidable Meech opponent who vowed his province would rescind ratification (which it did, in April 1990).

Yet with days to go before the expiry of the three-year deadline, the three so-called dissident premiers (and Manitoba's two opposition leaders) were coaxed into the fold by a so-called companion resolution, concocted by Mulroney and all ten premiers at an intense night-and-day meeting during the first week of June 1990. In exchange for agreeing to submit a resolution of ratification to their legislatures, the premiers accepted a statement of intentions on Senate reform and some down-the-road commitments: to "clarify" the distinct society clause's impact on the Charter; to set a House of Commons committee to work on creating a so-called Canada Clause embodying the country's fundamental characteristics; to hold a constitutional conference on aboriginal issues every three years; to tinker with Meech to strengthen such matters as the protection of sexual equality and to make it easier for the northern territories to enter the federation as provinces; and to involve the territories in Supreme Court appointments and first ministers' conferences.

The New Brunswick legislature, with all fifty-eight seats held by McKenna's Liberals, ratified the accord a week before the deadline. In Manitoba, however, the lone aboriginal member of the legislature, Elijah Harper, withheld the consent necessary to permit a ratification vote within the time allowed. Newfoundland's Clyde Wells submitted the resolution to the House of Assembly. But on hearing of the Accord's fate in Manitoba, he decided not to unnecessarily subject the province's legislators and citizens to a deeply divisive decision and adjourned the legislature without holding a vote. Thus the Meech Lake Accord died on June 23, 1990.

Quebec nationalists, with immediate happy enthusiasm, claimed that Quebec had been "humiliated" – a claim that throughout the three years of Meech had been encouraged by Mulroney and his cabinet members who had continuously told Canadians that a rejection of Meech meant a rejection of Quebec. Although nothing could have been further from the truth, the damage was done and another fallacious myth given birth (a baby brother to the myth that Quebec was "excluded" from the 1982 constitutional amendments). "The tragedy, of course," wrote historian Michael Bliss, "is that the Meech Lake fiasco bred tens, if not hundreds, of thousands of converts to Quebec's separatist revival." Conveniently forgotten was the fact that the Meech Lake Accord had been nearly as unpopular in Quebec as it was in the rest of the country.[*]

---

[*] A 1989 *Globe*–CBC poll showed only 33 per cent of Quebeckers were clearly in favour of the accord and 43 per cent did not know what to think. The *Globe and Mail* reported at the time: "These numbers could become Mr. Bourassa's nightmare. It is difficult to make a convincing case that Quebeckers would react strongly to a Meech failure when nearly half of them admit to a confused state of mind on the issue."

END-NOTES (1) – THE OKA CRISIS:
PURE-WOOL AUCHTOTONES
Within weeks of the death of Meech, Quebeckers woke to
nationalist fervour of a different sort. Aboriginal peoples,
encouraged by Elijah Harper's role in blocking the accord in
Manitoba, launched a national campaign for constitutional
recognition of aboriginal self-government. In the summer
of 1990, that campaign produced a sudden concrete manifestation in Oka, outside Montreal, where Mohawks set out
to stop expansion of a golf course on land they claimed
was theirs. Before the confrontation ended in September, a
Quebec policeman had been shot and Canadian troops called
in. The incident underscored the determination of aboriginal people not to let the federal government roll the dice on
their political and constitutional aspirations.

END-NOTES (2) – LOOKING FOR COMMON
GROUND, IF IT CAN BE CALLED THAT
The federal government, in the fall of 1990, created the
Citizens' Forum on Canada's Future (known as the Spicer
Commission after its chairman, Keith Spicer) to listen to
ordinary Canadians on what constitutional directions the
country should take. "They want consultation? We'll give
them consultation till it's coming out of their ears," said
Prime Minister Mulroney, perhaps not nicely. In any
event, the commission failed to generate much interest in
Quebec. Its June 1991 report, which confirmed that ordinary Canadians hated Meech Lake, hated the process that
created it, and wanted their national government and
national institutions to play a stronger role in Canada, was
entirely ignored by Mulroney's administration.

In January 1991, the Quebec Liberal party produced its constitutional position (the Allaire Report) which Premier Bourassa accurately described as recommending "Quebec autonomy within a federal structure." The report, by Montreal lawyer Jean Allaire, called for massive devolution of federal powers. Ottawa was to be left with responsibility for little more than national defence, the post office, and administering unconditional transfers to poorer provinces. (The opposition Parti Québécois, in predicting the rest of Canada would reject the Allaire Report, said it would mean another "humiliation" for Quebec.)

In March 1991, the Quebec National Assembly's Bélanger–Campeau Commission on Quebec's constitutional future recommended to the legislature that the rest of Canada be handed an ultimatum: it had until October 1992 to offer Quebec acceptable terms for a renewed federation; failing that, Quebeckers – "free to assume their own destiny, to determine their own political status and to ensure their own economic, social and cultural status" – might pursue sovereignty.

The Mulroney government, for its part, pursued timidity.

It deferred, in 1990, bringing into force new regulations under the Official Languages Act for fear of troubling the Quebec government, which had stated that it first had to vet any new federal programs to promote bilingualism and official-language minorities. It played only a desultory role in negotiations to reduce interprovincial barriers to commerce and to strengthen the economic union.

It concluded an immigration deal with Quebec which was a *de facto* act of Meechism – giving Quebec powers over the admission and integration of immigrants (although not refugees) and transferring an agreed-upon escalating amount of cash to Quebec for immigrant settlement. By 1995, under this agreement, Quebec was receiving 34 per cent of immigration-settlement funds while receiving only 19 per cent of immigrants. The agreement has no revocation clause; it can be altered, or ended, only by mutual consent – hardly likely on Quebec's side.

The Mulroney government also pursued a course that contributed to Canadians' sense of their country's fragility. It signed the U.S.–Canada Free Trade Agreement in the face of majority opposition (except in Quebec). It nurtured north–south economic links over east–west links. It began cutting funds to national institutions such as the CBC and Via Rail and to national programs like medicare, post-secondary education, and social assistance (through the Canada Assistance Plan).

Then, with many Canadians anxious about the prospects for their nation's survival, Mulroney set out to change the Constitution again.

CHAPTER 7

CHARLOTTETOWN:
MORE MORASS

On August 28 [1992], the apparently impossible was done. At Charlottetown, Brian Mulroney, ten premiers, two territorial leaders and leaders of the First Nations, the Métis and the Inuit were unanimous. A few days later, Brian Mulroney announced that, on October 26, all Canadians would have a chance to vote on the Charlottetown Accord in provincial or national referenda. The critics would have their turn. They were soon heard.
— Desmond Morton, "Strains of Affluence,"
Illustrated History of Canada

THE BÉLANGER–CAMPEAU ultimatum was given substance by Quebec legislation providing for a referendum on sovereignty. The federal government responded in the fall of 1991 by issuing twenty-eight "national unity proposals" (the newspeak for proposals for constitutional change) which in turn reignited the engines of pro-Meech politicians and their allies in journalism, academia, and business. All claimed to have learned two chastening lessons from Meech: one, that public participation had been insufficient and, two, that certain constituencies, notably aboriginals and women, had been left out. What they had not learned was Lesson Three: that the substance of Meech remained unacceptable. A majority of Canadians were opposed to the Meech vision of Canada, which diminished both the Charter and the federal government in favour of narrow provincialism and the country's further balkanization. Another year would pass until Lesson Three was absorbed – in the fall of 1992, when Canadians voted in a constitutional referendum on Son-of-Meech, the Charlottetown Constitutional Accord.

The road to Charlottetown was busy. A Special Joint Commons–Senate Committee on a Renewed Canada held hearings from September 1991 to February 1992. Aboriginal Hearings on the Constitution were held from September 1991 to spring 1992. Renewal-of-Canada conferences were held through the winter of 1991–92. Every provincial government and legislature held hearings, discussions, and conferences. Most reports took at least a year to complete. After four months of talks in seven cities, constitutional ministers from all governments except Quebec's – but including territorial and aboriginal negotiators – reached agreement on July 7, 1992, an agreement given the imprimatur of the first ministers (this time, the premier of Quebec among them) on August 28 in Charlottetown.

Within days, the Quebec government decided to ask its impending referendum question on the Charlottetown agreement rather than on sovereignty. The British Columbia and Alberta governments, as well, committed themselves to referendums. Soon Ottawa and the provinces decided that all Canadians should vote on the same question: "Do you agree that the Constitution of Canada should be renewed on the basis of the agreement reached on August 28?" A national referendum on the Charlottetown Accord was set for October 26, 1992.

The agreement's substance is here examined under five

broad headings: the Canada Clause, parliamentary reform, the division of powers, a social and economic union, and aboriginal self-government.

THE CANADA CLAUSE

Canada's Constitution, unlike those of many nations, is bereft of any preface containing noble sentiments about what the country stands for.* The authors of the Charlottetown Accord addressed this lacuna with the Canada Clause, an attempt to marry the intent of Meech – Quebec-as-a-distinct-society was retained, with considerably more muscle than it had before – with the aspirations of those who felt excluded by Meech. It listed eight "fundamental characteristics" of the country which would determine how the courts were to interpret the Constitution, including the Charter of Rights and Freedoms. The Canada Clause did not work; it made things worse. Here is the text:

1(a) Canada is a democracy committed to a parliamentary and federal system of government and to the rule of law;

1(b) The aboriginal peoples of Canada, being the first peoples to govern this land, have the right to promote their languages, cultures and traditions and to ensure

---

* If one discounts the droughty references to Canada "being founded upon principles that recognize the supremacy of God and the rule of law" (Constitution Act, 1982) and the authority of Queen and Parliament to make laws for "peace, order and good government" (Constitution Act, 1867).

the integrity of their societies, and their governments constitute one of three orders of government in Canada;

1(c) Quebec constitutes within Canada a distinct society, which includes a French-speaking majority, a unique culture and a civil law tradition;

1(d) Canadians and their governments are committed to the vitality and development of official-language minority communities throughout Canada;

1(e) Canadians are committed to racial and ethnic equality in a society that includes citizens from many lands who have contributed, and continue to contribute, to the building of a strong Canada that reflects its cultural and racial diversity;

1(f) Canadians are committed to a respect for individual and collective human rights and freedoms of all people;

1(g) Canadians are committed to the equality of female and male persons; and

1(h) Canadians confirm the principle of the equality of the provinces at the same time as recognizing their diverse characteristics.

(2) The role of the legislature and Government of Quebec to preserve and promote the distinct society of Quebec is affirmed.

(3) Nothing in this section derogates from the powers, rights or privileges of the Parliament or the Government of Canada, or of the legislatures or governments of the provinces, or of the legislative bodies or governments of the Aboriginal peoples of Canada, including any powers, rights or privileges relating to language and, for greater certainty, nothing in this section derogates from the aboriginal and treaty rights of the Aboriginal peoples of Canada.

It is readily apparent how Charlottetown made "distinct society" – with Sections 1(c) and 2 of the Canada Clause read together – more offensive than it had been in the Meech Accord. Charlottetown enlarged considerably on Meech's wording by giving the "distinct society" defined characteristics. In other words, the clause spelled out what one had to be in Quebec to be fully distinct – French-speaking and a member of French Quebec's "unique culture" – and then "affirmed" that the role of the legislature and government of Quebec was to "preserve and promote" those characteristics. With the Meech language, one could at least make the case that people of other cultures and languages who were resident in Quebec also were included in its distinctness. Not any more. This was profoundly unsettling for the hundreds of thousands of people who had immigrated to Quebec (over centuries) from other cultures, and had made important contributions to Quebec's social, cultural, legal, economic, and intellectual life.

In addition to the distinct society language, the Canada Clause stated that Canada is a parliamentary democracy, that aboriginal governments constitute one of three orders of government (along with federal and provincial, but not municipal government), and that Canadians respect official-language minority communities, ethnic and gender equality, and collective human rights.

The reference to "collective rights" picked off the scab on all the old concerns about "special status" and constitutionalized different orders of Canadians. The reference was especially troubling in light of the clause's anemic support for most of the other characteristics of Canada. Note, in particular, the passive responsibility accorded to the federal government and other provinces vis-à-vis official-language minorities in contrast to the unambiguous constitutional powers to preserve and promote a distinct society given the Quebec government. Critics of the Canada Clause said it created both a hierarchy of rights and a "new tribalism." For example, "racial and ethnic equality" took precedence over all other characteristics of Canada except the rule of law and government, aboriginal culture, and Quebec distinct society, and so would count for more before the courts than other aspects of human identity such as gender. As for persons left off the list altogether – for example, the disabled – they might well feel as if they counted for nothing. The obvious problem with the use of a list is that any group not listed is by inference excluded.

PARLIAMENTARY REFORM

The Charlottetown Accord proposed a form of Triple-E (equal, elected, effective) Senate.

It would be equal. There would be six senators from each province, two from each territory, and some potential aboriginal representation. This, in total, would reduce the number of existing senators by forty-two. Charlottetown provided for the House Commons to be enlarged by forty-two seats. Partly in recognition of its reduced representation in the new Senate, Quebec was to be assured a minimum 25 per cent of the seats in the Commons. This provision, however innocuous it might have proved to be, served as a lightning rod for hostility elsewhere in the country, particularly in British Columbia, which was at the time, and still is, one of the fastest-growing regions in the country and already felt underrepresented in the Commons.

It would be elected, sort of. Its members would be either popularly elected or elected by provincial legislatures, the latter in effect meaning appointment by any government having majority control of its legislature. The Quebec government immediately indicated it would elect the province's senators through the legislature.

Would it be effective? The Charlottetown Accord took away the Senate's (rarely exercised) power to amend or reject ordinary legislation emanating from the Commons. If the Senate amended or voted against an ordinary Commons bill, the legislation would be sent to a joint sitting of both Houses, and there submitted to a combined vote of both Senate and Commons members. If the Senate amended or voted against Commons legislation involving revenue and taxation, the Commons would need to wait only thirty days and then vote on the measure again, at which point it would be Senate-proof. The Senate could kill Commons legislation dealing with "fundamental tax policy changes directly related to natural resources." The argument in this case was that, because the provinces own the natural resources within their boundaries, they should have substantial authority over how those resources are taxed. Had this provision been in place in 1980, the National Energy Policy would likely have been blocked.

Legislation "materially affecting French language or French culture" would require approval by a double majority in the Senate; that is, by a majority of all senators present and by a majority of francophone senators present. Any dispute over whether a bill fell into this category would be settled by the Speaker of the Senate. Finally, the Senate would gain a new power to approve (or reject) government nominations for the governor of the Bank of Canada, the heads of national cultural institutions (such as the CBC), and the heads of federal regulatory boards and agencies (such as the National Energy Board). A simple majority would prevail.

Critics of Charlottetown's Senate reforms asked how effective the proposed chamber really would be, given that it would rarely have the numbers to influence the outcome of a combined parliamentary vote on ordinary legislation. As for the double-majority condition attached to legislation affecting French language and culture, this would leave the Quebec government with a *de facto* veto over federal law in these areas – touching on everything from national museums to international cultural relations, from official bilingualism to multicultural programs. Why a veto? Because most francophone senators would come from Quebec, and their "election" by Quebec's National Assembly would in reality be appointment by the provincial government of the day. In fact, enough senators appointed by a separatist Quebec government could have the means of dismantling bilingualism in Canada.

With respect to the amending formula, Charlottetown followed in the footsteps of Meech by adding to the list of constitutional topics that would require unanimous consent from Parliament and the ten provincial legislatures in order for them to be changed. Under Charlottetown, the list was expanded to include further alterations to the Senate, any changes to the House of Commons (including the proposed guarantee to Quebec of a minimum 25 per cent of Commons seats) and changes to the role and composition of the Supreme Court. Charlottetown followed Meech in proposing the nomination of Supreme Court judges from provincial lists, a process that would remain subject to the general amending formula.) New provinces could be admitted to the federation by bilateral agreement with Ottawa, but their status vis-à-vis various amending formulas and the numbers of senators they would be allowed would require constitutional approval under the unanimity rule.

Charlottetown also followed Meech in authorizing reasonable compensation for any province opting out from constitutional amendments affecting the federal–provincial division of powers.

THE DIVISION OF POWERS

The Charlottetown Accord provided for a great deal of central power being devolved to all provinces. This was preferred to asymmetrical federalism – that is, different powers being given to different provinces, save, of course, for Quebec's distinct-society guarantee.

Meech Lake's restrictions on the spending power made it into the Charlottetown Accord *in toto*. If a province did not like the federal model for a new program in which the spending power was to be exercised, it could take the federal money and run, so long as it offered an alternative program which met the "national objectives" (this was called "opting out with compensation"). As noted in the previous chapter, this provision would effectively preclude the establishment of minimum national standards and hand the provinces a massive disincentive to join with the federal government in pursuing important national social-policy and equity-adjustment goals.

The federal power of disallowance over provincial legislation was formally dropped. The federal government agreed to abandon jurisdiction in six areas – the so-called Six Sisters – where both Ottawa and the provinces historically had been active: forestry, mining, tourism, housing, recreation, and municipal and urban affairs. Intergovernmental agreements would spell out how the federal government withdrew from these matters: provincial governments would be given authority to prevent direct federal spending in these areas, to specify transfer of federal financial resources, or, alternatively, to demand that federal spending be maintained. Federal jurisdiction for culture would be strictly limited to "Canadian cultural matters" and include responsibility for national institutions such as the CBC and federal agencies that fund cultural activities in the provinces (e.g., the Canada Council). Otherwise, the provinces would have exclusive jurisdiction over all cultural matters within their borders. Ottawa would retain responsibility for unemployment insurance and job creation but would have to surrender labour-market training to those provinces which wanted exclusive authority over it. In immigration, one of the two original areas of shared federal–provincial jurisdiction that have existed since 1867 (the other is agriculture), the federal government would be obliged to negotiate – with any province at that province's request – immigration agreements outlining provincial authority

Not surprisingly, this devolution of powers was strongly opposed during the referendum campaign. The Spicer Commission had found that most Canadians rejected further decentralization of their already decentralized federation and were angered by their politicians talking incessantly about trading legislative responsibilities without articulating precisely what they wanted to do with them or how possessing them would advance the public interest. Quebec political scientist (and now federal cabinet minister) Stéphane Dion pointed out that most Quebeckers had never been concerned about the transfer of powers between Ottawa and Quebec as an end in itself.* Quebeckers were at least as critical of their provincial services as were other Canadians. For instance, at the very time that Quebec's constitutional negotiators were insisting on federal withdrawal from worker-training and manpower fields, Quebec business leaders were rejecting the Quebec government's own recently revealed strategy in this area. On culture and language, Montreal novelist Pierre Billon (writing in *L'Actualité*, December 1991) asked:

> If our language is in danger, how is it possible to explain the poverty of [Quebec] government action to protect it? ... Our politicians declare that our cultural identity is threatened, but this threat doesn't seem to them all that serious, if one is to judge by the modest spending and weak programs for arts and culture. ...

---

* He nevertheless supported the Charlottetown Accord.

It is claimed that the powers that Quebec has under
the existing constitution are insufficient to protect its
cultural specificity. *The politicians who make these
arguments would be more convincing if they were to
exercise fully the powers they already have before asking
for new ones* [emphasis ours].

The devolution of powers revealed an absence of any
coherent national vision. The Charlottetown Accord would
have permitted a confusing mix of bilateral and multilateral
federal–provincial agreements in a wide range of areas, and
their entrenchment – however complex they might be – in
the Constitution. This would have resulted not only in a
patchwork quilt of different provincial legislative powers,
but also confusing lines of accountability and little sense of
common purpose. It would have generated an uncontrolled
and incoherent asymmetry in powers, wreaking havoc on the
economic union. (As it was, Ottawa failed to get the provincial governments to harmonize their economic programs
and eliminate trade barriers in the interests of strengthening a Canadian common market.)

The fact that these federal–provincial agreements might
automatically expire at the end of five years and require the
legislatures concerned to renew them would not change this
assessment. Once responsibility for policy has shifted, it is
likely to be politically impossible for the federal government to recover it: after five years provincial bureaucracies
and vested interests would be deeply entrenched. The constitutional entrenchment of complex agreements – including detailed funding formulas – would quickly lead to the
constitution becoming as incomprehensible as the Income
Tax Act. The role of federal MPs from provinces having

complete jurisdiction over certain policy areas would certainly be called into question. Eventually, Parliament could become unworkable – a hodgepodge body with different classes of MPs, different voting authorities, and so on. This is what asymmetrical federalism means. In all cases, the federal government and Parliament would be weakened in fundamentally unaccountable and undemocratic ways involving behind-the-scenes horse trading and brokering between governments.

At the Charlottetown conference and in their later public pronouncements, first ministers gave few clear indications of which specific policies and laws would shift from the federal to the provincial level under these agreements and what the implications would be for ordinary citizens. In the case of the termination of federal jurisdiction in housing and urban affairs, for example, was it intended that the provinces have the legal right to dismantle the Canada Mortgage and Housing Corporation or insist that the federal government withdraw from the provision of low-cost housing to Canadians? This was never spelled out. Equally ambiguous was the impact of ending federal jurisdiction in such environmentally sensitive industries as forestry and mining. Would the federal government also be required to abandon its role of environmental protection in these industries? Also, since these industries represent a substantial portion of Canada's exports, what would be the implications for the federal power over international trade and related industrial policy?

Similarly, what would be the real impact of shifting "culture" into the almost exclusive jurisdiction of the provinces – when no one knows the limits to the meaning of "culture." Queen's University law professor Dan Soberman

noted that some cultural claims advanced by even supposedly moderate Quebec nationalists – that the Great Whale
hydro-electric project in northern Quebec was vital to the
province's future cultural security, for example – threatened
to encompass "the whole of economic policy." And while the
Supreme Court of Canada probably would not go that far in
interpreting the meaning of "culture," it is likely that Quebec
nationalists, in response, would claim another "betrayal"
of their expectations from renewed federalism. Would
we give them even more powers to appease them? Would we
once again risk break-up and separation? Here again, we see
how the Charlottetown Accord would have refurnished the
stage for permanent constitutional warfare.

At the very least, the accord would have obstructed any
coherent national cultural policy. Since there was no guid-
ance as to how to distinguish cultural matters "within the
province" from so-called "Canadian" cultural matters, much
of cultural policy would have been tied up for years in contentious constitutional litigation. These implications were
not thought through in the rush to get a deal.

Similarly, little analysis was made of the exclusion of
federal jurisdiction with respect to labour-market development and training. The productivity and skills base of the
national labour force are an essential source of national
competitive advantage. Explicitly excluding the federal
government from the training field would make it difficult,
if not impossible, for long-needed reforms to replace pro-
duction subsidies, trade restrictions, and other inefficient
federal policies with adjustment-oriented measures aimed at
giving workers the capacity to find work outside depressed
industries or regions. The provisions of the Charlottetown

Accord did pay some lip-service to a federal role. It contemplated that the federal government be allowed, in the case of labour-market training provisions, to set "national policy objectives." But it remained unclear from the text whether these objectives would even apply in provinces that opted for complete federal withdrawal from a given field, and it is noted that, in the Quebec Liberal party's public explanation of the accord's labour-market training provisions, all mention of national objectives was missing. Moreover, where provinces did not choose to exercise their exclusive jurisdiction, the accord would give them the right to constrain federal spending through court-enforced bilateral agreements. Thus, in sum, instead of getting on with the pressing task of, say, retraining workers for global competition, governments (and unions) would end up arguing in court about whether provincial policies met national objectives, about how much money each province was entitled to receive from the federal treasury, and about whether one province's bilateral deal was sweeter than another's.

The accord did retain formal federal authority over unemployment insurance, but only with respect to income support and related matters. Hence, the federal government would have been prevented from creatively restructuring unemployment insurance to help develop workers' skills or serve other important goals related to the special needs of women and disabled people in the workplace. In addition, the federal government would have been required to enter into agreements with the provinces concerning "administrative arrangements" pertaining to unemployment insurance.

In a different way, but with the same results, the federal power in respect of immigration was also significantly reduced. As with the Meech Accord, all provinces would henceforth be able to require that Ottawa conclude an agreement on immigration. Thus, just at the moment when Canada required a coherent national immigration policy to help meet the demographic challenge of its ageing population, Charlottetown raised the spectre of eleven (federal and provincial) different and competing immigration policies and a severe weakening of the federal role in providing new Canadians with a sense of belonging to Canada.

In general, it could be argued that the vague provisions sprinkled throughout the Charlottetown Accord for the federal government to provide financial compensation to provinces when transferring jurisdictions under intergovernmental agreements were the height of fiscal irresponsibility. Taxpayers of Canada would have been forced to fund a vast range of unaccountable provincial programs and activities, something that would have seriously impaired Parliament's ability to allocate tax revenues according to the democratic will of the Canadian people. What kind of compensation was being required? A one-shot payment to the provinces, or a perpetual charge on the federal treasury? The authors of the Charlottetown Accord didn't say.

Initially, in defending its give-away of powers to the provinces, the federal government maintained that its own activities in these areas involved waste and duplication. If this was so, then it was mystifying why the provinces should have to be compensated for them.

One final note on the division of powers. Supporters of the accord continually claimed that the devolution of federal powers to the provinces brought government closer to the people and avoided overlap and duplication. Opponents, on the other hand, queried how much closer government

was brought to the people through complex intergovernmental agreements, negotiated behind closed doors and put
in place without the scrutiny provided by the process of
formal constitutional amendments. They queried, as well,
how much closer government was brought to the people
through provincial middlemen spending federal money.
When Ottawa works with business and labour to retrain
steelworkers to meet the challenges of global competition,
or when it provides grants directly to multicultural groups
or to a women's shelter, then the national government is
brought closer to the people. Why have a provincial bureaucracy in between?

THE SOCIAL AND ECONOMIC UNION

Ontario's New Democratic government of the time led a
campaign for a "social charter" that would strengthen the
country through a national commitment to social programs and goals that would have legally guaranteed every
Canadian a certain standard of living. The social charter was
a non-starter at Charlottetown and was quickly pushed off
the table. The Charlottetown Accord offered instead a set of
broadly defined social principles that could not be judicially
enforced. The principles would have been monitored by an
agency to be established in the future. They included universal health care, social programs and benefits, education,
workers' rights, and environmental protection. Like so much
else in the accord, this proposal was criticized by various
groups as being either too weak or too strong. As for the
economic union, Ottawa, as mentioned above, failed to win
provincial agreement to strengthen the Canadian "common
market," to harmonize provincial and federal economic

programs, and to eliminate interprovincial trade barriers. Instead, Ottawa settled for a mere statement of policy objectives committing governments to the principle of a common market. Ottawa's weakness vis-à-vis the provinces was all too evident.

ABORIGINAL SELF-GOVERNMENT

At Confederation, the constitutional rights of aboriginal peoples were left – to say the least – undefined, uncertain, and subsequently subject to widely varying interpretations. The Constitution Act, 1867 states only that Indians and Indian lands are under federal jurisdiction. Because of this constitutional vacuum, the rights of aboriginal people have been defined by a combination of written treaties, common-law traditions, court rulings, pre-Confederation pledges such as the Royal Proclamation of 1763, and ordinary federal laws such as the Indian Act. In summing up this pastiche of citations, Hogg writes: "it seems likely that the aboriginal peoples of Canada held rights of some kind with respect to the lands that they occupied at the time of European settlement, and that those rights, unless voluntarily surrendered or taken away by statute, survived the reception of French and English law that occurred as the result of European settlement."

Under a typical treaty, says Hogg, "an Indian tribe would cede land to the Crown, and the Crown would promise in return to set aside particular areas as Indian reserves, to make annual payments and grant other supplies to the Indians, and to permit hunting and fishing throughout the surrendered land." Some aboriginal peoples, such as the Iroquois nations of central Canada and the Treaty 6 and 7 bands of Alberta and Saskatchewan, were convinced that their historical treaties are a guarantee of their sovereignty. Yet for most of the nineteenth and twentieth centuries, the federal government took the opposite view: it believed that any so-called rights of aboriginal peoples could be extinguished by the stroke of a pen or, more precisely, by the vote of a legislature. Thus, for example, until 1951, federal laws prohibited Indians from practising their traditional spiritual beliefs. This notion stemmed from what Hogg calls the three "infirmities" of the aboriginals' situation: first, the relationship of aboriginals to the land and the treaties themselves lacked close analogies in the common law; secondly, the doctrine of parliamentary sovereignty was interpreted to mean that any aboriginal "rights" were subject to the whim of the constitutionally competent legislature; and, thirdly, the concept of "equality," which gained increasing acceptance in Canada after the Second World War, was unsympathetic to any notion of special status.

The federal government came to be convinced otherwise by key Supreme Court of Canada rulings in the 1970s stating that aboriginal fishing and hunting rights are free from provincial regulation. Thus two important provisions dealing with aboriginal rights were included in the Constitution Act, 1982. Section 35 "recognized and affirmed" the "existing aboriginal and treaty rights" of Canada's native people. Those rights were not defined, but Section 25 of the Charter pointed to where a definition might be found and offered constitutional weight to the definition:

The guarantee in this Charter of certain rights and freedoms shall not be construed so as to abrogate or derogate from any aboriginal treaty or other rights

or freedoms that pertain to the aboriginal peoples of
Canada including

(a) any rights or freedoms that have been recognized by the Royal Proclamation of October 7, 1763;
and
(b) any rights or freedoms that may be acquired
by the aboriginal peoples of Canada by way of land
claims settlement.

The Constitution Act, 1982 also required that three constitutional conferences be held on the issue. The third, ending
in March 1987 just before the conclusion of the Meech Lake
Accord, brought no resolution. Indeed, aboriginal frustration and resentment only deepened as aboriginal issues
were tossed aside in favour of the politicians' enthusiastic
pursuit of the so-called Quebec Round of negotiations. It
was this frustration that led aboriginal MLA Elijah Harper,
to block ratification of the Meech Accord in the Manitoba
legislature and, a few weeks later, to militant action by angry
Mohawks in Oka, Quebec.

The Charlottetown Accord attempted to accommodate
the aspirations of aboriginal peoples, as the 1982 constitutional amendments intended. It was the first clear declaration of the aboriginal right to self-government. It established
that this right is "inherent" – meaning it has always existed
and was not to be construed as a gift from federal and provincial governments (a principle the first ministers accepted
on assurance that self-government had no international
dimension, that is, no notion of a separate sovereignty
within a Canadian state). The accord stated that aboriginal
governments would be considered "one of three orders

of government in Canada." The governments of aboriginal people would have the authority to "safeguard and develop their languages, cultures, economies, identities and traditions" and to "develop, maintain and strengthen their relationship with their lands, water and environment."

Several so-called political accords committed government and aboriginal peoples to negotiating the details. If there was deadlock, or no resolution, on individual negotiations after five years, claims could be taken to the courts for final determination.

The impact of this provision would have varied enormously from community to community. Some communities, such as the James Bay Cree of northern Quebec, have already achieved a large measure of self-government as a result of negotiations with Ottawa and the provinces. An aboriginal majority already controls the existing Legislative Council of the Northwest Territories. In 1999, the new, Inuit-controlled territory of Nunavut will be carved out of the N.W.T., with Inuktitut as the proposed official language of government. Elsewhere, reserves are at various stages along the road to control of their own schools, child-welfare agencies, health clinics, social programs, and other local institutions, together with their own justice systems and police forces and so forth. Native communities in major cities are seeking their own forms of self-government.

And yet Charlottetown's self-government proposals were controversial among aboriginals as much as they were among Canadians generally. In separate referendum votes on reserves, they were defeated more often than accepted. The major problem was the relationship between the Charlottetown proposals and the Charter. The accord stated that the Charter is "to apply immediately to governments

of aboriginal peoples," but – and a very big "but" this was
– it then proposed to give the legislative bodies of aboriginal peoples access to the Charter's notwithstanding, or
override, clause without specifying if or how those bodies
were to be elected. Of equal concern, a strengthened non-
derogation clause would allow aboriginal governments to
escape Charter obligations altogether when the "exercise
or protection of their languages, culture or traditions" was
at issue. Thus, many aboriginal women were frightened by
the aboriginal package's absence of any commitment to
entrenched Charter rights, including gender rights.

Indeed, a unanimous ruling by the Federal Court of
Appeal, made public one week before the first ministers and
aboriginal leaders announced the Charlottetown Accord on
August 28, 1992, stated that aboriginal women (represented
by the Native Women's Association of Canada) had had their
Charter right to freedom of expression violated by being
denied a seat at the constitutional negotiating table. In the
court's view, the heavily male-dominated aboriginal groups
given a place at the table – the Native Council of Canada,
the Assembly of First Nations, the Inuit Tapirisat, and the
Métis National Council – inadequately represented aboriginal women and their interests. In delivering the court's
judgment, Mr. Justice P.M. Mahoney quoted at length from
a native woman's brief:

Aboriginal women are at a crisis point. The government of Canada is funding advocacy for a point of
view that will, if successful, see the removal from
Aboriginal women of their rights under the Charter
of Rights and Freedoms. . . . As an Aboriginal woman,
I face the prospect that the price I will pay for

Aboriginal self-government will be the loss of my existing equality rights. . . . Why are we so worried as women? We have never discussed self-governments in our communities. There is much to be learned. We are living in chaos in our communities. We have a disproportionately high rate of child sexual abuse and incest. We have wife batterings, gang rapes, drug and alcohol abuse and every kind of perversion imaginable has been imported in our daily lives. The development of programs, services and policies for handling domestic violence has been placed in the hands of men. Has it resulted in a woman or child safe in their own home in an Aboriginal community? The statistics show this is not the case.

It was, alas, a moot, after-the-fact judgment.

THE REFERENDUM ITSELF

The Charlottetown referendum campaign was a rough and tough affair. Prime Minister Mulroney started out by calling opponents of the accord "enemies of Canada." Rather than focussing on the accord's substance, he emphasized the irreparable damage to the economy, if not the integrity of the country, that would result from a "no" vote. He and others met initial demands that Canadians be allowed to see the legal text before voting with suggestions that most voters would not understand what the wording meant. When the legal text was finally released on October 9, it was evident that many contentious points had been camouflaged by ambiguous wording. For example, paragraph 2(1)(h) of the Canada Clause, which read: "Canada confirms the principle of equality of the provinces at the same time as recognizing their diverse characteristics." Meaning what? Moreover, an analysis of the text determined that the accord contained no fewer than forty-eight points that were subject to "political accords" or future first ministers' negotiations.

On October 26, most Canadians said No. In Newfoundland, New Brunswick, Prince Edward Island, and Ontario, the result was virtually an even split. In Quebec, 55 per cent voted No, as did a narrow majority in Nova Scotia. Across the West, the accord was resoundingly defeated. Lesson Three had come home to roost: the substance of Meech, recloaked as Charlottetown, remained unacceptable. A majority of Canadians remained opposed to the Meech vision of Canada, which diminished both the Charter and the federal government in favour of narrow provincialism and the country's further balkanization. But had they really learned, the Meech politicians and their allies?

SECTION 43: BACK DOOR TO
MEECH AND CHARLOTTETOWN

In the spring of 1993, several months after the defeat of the Charlottetown Accord, the federal government proceeded with a bilateral constitutional amendment with New Brunswick to entrench the equality of status of the French and English *communities* in the province, an amendment eventually set in concrete by means of the bilateral amending formula (Section 43[b]) of the Constitution Act, 1982. This stated that:

> An amendment to the Constitution of Canada in relation to any provision that applies to one or more, but

not all, provinces . . . that relates to the use of the English or the French language within a province may be made by proclamation issued by the Governor-General . . . where so authorized by resolutions of the Senate and the House of Commons and of the legislative assembly of each province to which the amendment applies.

The academic and media elites praised the amendment as a laudable step to strengthen the status of its francophones and the French language in the province. They also saw it as the harbinger of a bright future for the bilateral amending formula – something that could, and should, be stretched to the maximum to circumvent the barriers of the seemingly impossible general amending (7-50) and unanimity formulas. What they refused to recognize were the serious concerns about the propriety of using the bilateral formula for this particular amendment.

Section 43 was clearly intended by its legislative authors to be used for narrowly focussed amendments that affect only one province.[*] The bilateral New Brunswick amendment did more than this; it had implications beyond the province's boundaries. It fundamentally altered the Charter guarantees of individual rights and freedoms by promoting the power of communities, by introducing the alien notion of collective rights (as well as extending a special role to the

---

[*] Section 43 was never intended as a general amending short-cut. It had a precise purpose: the amendment of province-specific provisions falling – and already existing – within the "Constitution of Canada." Subsection 43(b), among other things, was aimed at permitting other provinces to join New Brunswick by declaring themselves officially bilingual.

New Brunswick government to protect those collective rights) – which is precisely what the Canadian people said No to in the Meech Lake and Charlottetown accords. At the very least, such an amendment should have required the authorization of the 7-50 formula. As we have noted earlier, minority language and education rights in the Charter, as well as the rights in New Brunswick relating to its "officially bilingual" status, belong not to groups, but to individuals, and to exercise these rights one need not be a member of any group or submit to any distinct society. The Charter prior to the bilateral amendment provided that anyone may use either English or French in legislative debates in New Brunswick and in the courts. The Charter provided, as well, that "any member of the public" has the right to communicate with the New Brunswick government and receive services from that government in either English or French.

The bilateral amendment has the effect of transferring power from individuals to the French and English "communities" – or collectives – which are declared to have equality of status and the right to distinct institutions. The New Brunswick government and legislature are then given the special legislative status to "promote" these distinct institutions and their power over "culture" is affirmed, something which is most certainly not assigned to the provinces in the Constitution.

Supporters of the amendment argue that it will increase linguistic freedom, and that it merely represents the constitutional entrenchment of existing provincial legislation, enabling the francophone communities to control their own institutions. The latter is certainly desirable, but it was subject to the Charter's guarantees of individual rights and freedoms: no one was forced to be part of a collectivity to assert their language and education rights. Everyone was free to choose his or her own allies or associates among either anglophones or francophones.

What the bilateral amendment implies – strongly – is that the individual's right to linguistic, cultural, and educational choice depends on him or her being defined as a member of one or the other collectivity. And if it is the group, not the individual, who holds the rights, who exactly are the people with the authority to speak for all members of the group? And who has the power to enforce those rights? The amendment is silent on all this. Must the group's representatives – whoever they are – be elected by each community? Can these representatives who control the distinctive institutions decide, for example, who counts and who does not count as a member of, say, the French community, and who, therefore, can partake of community rights? What about mixed marriages, or francophones who do not count as members of the Acadian cultural grouping by birth? What about people who have come to New Brunswick from cultures other than English or French and hence do not have a right to "distinct cultural institutions"? Do they become second-class citizens with no claim on the state whatever to preserve their non-English, non-French cultural identity? Does the right to "distinct educational institutions" or "distinct cultural institutions" include the right to exclude from these institutions anyone who fails the appropriate ethnic test? All of these questions remain unanswered. And yet the elites were jubilant at the Section 43 amendment.

Until its legality is challenged, the amendment stands as a precedent for a broad interpretation of the Section 43 bilateral formula. Indeed, proposals since then have been

brought forward for bilateral amendments under Section 43
to give Quebec distinct-society status, even to give provinces control over language and culture on an individual
basis. Fortunately, the federal government has not pursued
them (at least officially), and it would be advisable to obtain
a Supreme Court ruling on the scope of Section 43 before
proceeding further with similar amendments.

SECTION 43: USED PROPERLY
Shortly after the New Brunswick amendment was approved,
Section 43 was appropriately used in early 1994 to amend the
Terms of Union of Prince Edward Island to allow for a fixed
link – a bridge – as a substitute for ferry service between the
island and the mainland (the ferry service having been guaranteed in the province's Terms of Union). In the spring of
1996, a bilateral amendment altering Newfoundland's Terms
of Union concerning denominational education was also
properly passed. Opponents, who were very vocal, argued
that the amendment could not be done bilaterally because
it affected "minority rights," something that was difficult to
sustain, especially when the largest group in opposition, the
Roman Catholic Church, was in fact in a majority position
in the province.

Similarly, Quebec finally requested, and the federal government agreed, in 1997 to a bilateral amendment permitting
the Quebec government to end the 1867 guarantee of denominational (Protestant or Roman Catholic) school boards for
Montreal and Quebec City. This had the effect of simplifying
Quebec's reorganization of its school-board system, from the
historical religious basis to a linguistic basis.

Both Newfoundland's and Quebec's amendments fall legitimately within the intentions of Section 43, since they involve province-specific constitutional provisions and, unlike the New Brunswick bilateral amendment, did not have an impact on the fundamental structure of the Charter (and therefore on other Canadians in other provinces).

In the Quebec case, the federal government did take the opportunity to note that the Parti Québécois government was effectively accepting the existing Canadian Constitution – specifically, the Constitution Act, 1982 – by requesting the bilateral amendment. However, it did not go further and insist that the Quebec government formally acknowledge this fact. A good opportunity to counter nationalist myths was lost. Alas, as will be discussed in the next chapter, the Meech–Charlottetown mentality continues to dominate federal constitutional thinking.

CHAPTER 8

MINDSETS IN
CONCRETE, BUT . . .

There is no reason for discouragement.
—W.L. Grant, *Ontario High School*
History of Canada (1992)

CONTRARY TO BRIAN MULRONEY's prediction – and that
of many others who misunderstood the country – Canada
did not fall apart when the Charlottetown Accord was
defeated. Its political face, however, changed. Canadians made
clear they no longer wanted to talk about the Constitution.
Economic and social uncertainties in Canada were far too
pressing and had been too much neglected by the politicians with their constitutional obsession – uncertainties
and obsession which, together, created an alchemy for
transformation.

In the first half of 1993, the Mulroney government tried
Meech and Charlottetown by the back door – employing
administrative tools to accede to some of the Quebec government's demands. After Meech, it will be recalled, the
Mulroney government had made a bilateral immigration
deal with Quebec. Following Charlottetown, it reached a
bilateral agreement in principle to transfer jurisdiction over
labour market training to Quebec (a similar arrangement

was made with New Brunswick a month later). But implementation was slow, and the federal election arrived before the deals were set in concrete.

The public-opinion polls in advance of the election showed Mulroney to be the most unpopular prime minister in Canadian polling history. The Conservatives changed leaders, bringing Kim Campbell onstage as Canada's first female head of government. The national vote, in October 1993, destroyed the party; only two Conservative members of Parliament were elected (Campbell not among them). The void left by the Tories was filled by two regional protest groups, the Western neo-conservative Reform Party and the separatist Bloc Québécois. Astonishingly, the Bloc, committed to the destruction of Canada, became the official loyal opposition.

Liberal leader Jean Chrétien, the new prime minister, indicated his government would not proceed with the bilateral labour-market agreement. Rather, he pledged to work with the provinces to create single access points to federal and provincial employment, job-training, and counselling services ("one-stop shopping"). Ottawa also invited provincial governments to play a role in planning federal job-training programs, and to manage retraining programs purchased by the federal government from private agencies. The first agreement under these proposals was reached with Saskatchewan in late 1994. The proposals were dismissed as inadequate by Quebec's Liberal government, and then by its Parti Québécois successor, elected on September 15, 1994. The PQ government, under Jacques Parizeau, was not interested in any federal flexibility on constitutional powers. It withdrew from the federal–provincial committee established to harmonize initiatives by the two levels of government in areas of joint jurisdiction. It requested federal withdrawal from a joint forest-management agreement for eastern Quebec, and it asserted sole provincial responsibility for major aspects of fishery management.

UDI AND THE BIG QUESTION: CAN QUEBEC SIMPLY LEAVE?

While he held the federal government at bay with his left hand, with his right hand Parizeau set about preparing the way for the creation of an independent Quebec. In December 1994, his government made public a draft bill (An Act Respecting the Sovereignty of Quebec) authorizing a unilateral declaration of independence (UDI) within a year of a majority vote favouring Quebec sovereignty being obtained in a provincial referendum. The bill authorized the provincial government to negotiate a Quebec–Canada economic association. It stipulated that Quebec's existing boundaries would be retained; that residents of Quebec holding Canadian citizenship would acquire concurrent Quebec citizenship; and that the Canadian dollar would be the official currency of Quebec.

The UDI proposal was not popular in Quebec. Thus, ten months later, on September 7, 1995, the Parizeau government introduced another bill in the National Assembly: An Act Respecting the Future of Quebec. This bill required that a "formal offer of economic and political partnership" be made to Canada before any proclamation of UDI by the National Assembly. It also declared that Quebeckers would vote on October 30 on the following referendum question:

Do you agree that Quebec becomes sovereign after having made a formal offer to Canada of a new economic and political partnership within the context of the Bill on the future of Quebec and the agreement signed on June 12, 1995? [The agreement referred to is one negotiated among the PQ, the Bloc Québécois, and the new party, l'Action démocratique du Québec, begun by nationalists who had earlier broken away from the Quebec Liberal party.]

THE OCTOBER 1995 REFERENDUM

The federalists believed that a No vote would prevail as long as it was made clear to Quebeckers that a Yes meant sovereignty, pure and simple. Accordingly, the federalist side consistently warned that Yes would mean separation from Canada and a grim economic future. The federalists had very little positive to say about Canada. One commentator observed: "The no side ... could make no better case for the federation than to list the many ways in which it has become irrelevant to Quebec: The province runs its own pension fund, collects its own tax, sends squadrons of ambassadors abroad, and on and on." The arguments of cataclysmic economic doom had little impact, and when, in mid-October, the charismatic Bloc Québécois leader Lucien Bouchard with his powerful emotional appeals for a sovereign Quebec took over the Yes campaign from Jacques Parizeau, the No side finally realized it was in trouble.

A full 94 per cent of eligible voters cast their ballots. The margin between the Yes and No sides was only 53,000 votes – less than 1 per cent.

On the night of the vote, after it became clear that the

separatists had narrowly lost, Parizeau angrily blamed "money and the ethnic vote" for the defeat, an outrageous comment that precipitated his sudden departure from politics and his replacement as premier by Lucien Bouchard in February 1996.

Many francophone commentators dismissed Parizeau's comment – as on other occasions they have dismissed "Anglos go home" graffiti and rocks thrown through the windows of English stores – as a marginal, isolated event. They argued that Parizeau's comments were not representative and that Quebec nationalism was not ethnocentric.

Yet there cannot be any doubt that there is a vocal, articulate minority of Quebeckers – *pure laine* Quebeckers (descendants of the original French settlers) whose predecessors were the disciples of Lionel Groulx – who see Quebec nationalism as ethnically based, as an issue of "us" versus "them." These include PQ adviser Pierre Bourgault, who called on non-francophones to refrain from voting in the October referendum for fear of a backlash if the separatists lost by a small margin. They also include those Quebeckers who publicly advocated, during the hearings on the Act Respecting the Future of Quebec, that only the "pure" French should participate in the referendum.

Action inevitably leads to reaction. During the summer of 1996, an anglophone Montreal advertising executive, Howard Galganov, emerged as a populist leader demanding that stores put up bilingual signs (albeit with French predominant), a step permitted since the expiry in 1993 of the Quebec government's legal authority under the notwithstanding clause to violate constitutional language and freedom-of-expression protections. The actions of Galganov and others make clear that English-speaking Quebeckers are increasingly disillusioned with their federalist political leaders in both Ottawa and Quebec City and are taking matters into their own hands. Meanwhile, their numbers continue to shrink. A recent poll showed 30 per cent of English-speaking Quebeckers – 40 per cent of those between the ages of eighteen and thirty-four – intend to be living elsewhere in five years' time.

THE PARTITION ISSUE

Since the referendum, the federal government has found ways of showing a harder face to the separatists – Plan B, in Ottawaspeak. It has taken a tougher stance on the legality of secession (see the *Bertrand* case, below) and has supported the growing movement favouring the partition of Quebec in the event of UDI and separation.

The possibility of partition was first raised during the 1980 referendum. At that time, a group of anglophone Quebeckers argued that, if a segment of the province's population in, say, a defined section of Montreal preferred to remain Canadian, they should be allowed to separate from a sovereign Quebec. In the intervening years, the notion has been kept alive in the Montreal area (at least twenty municipal councils, most of them in and around greater Montreal, have passed resolutions indicating their desire to remain in Canada) as well as embraced by aboriginal peoples living in northern Quebec (whose territory was annexed by Ottawa to Quebec after Confederation; see below). The thesis reflects both logic and justice: if Quebec claims the right to secede from Canada, then Quebec must recognize a similar right in favour of identifiable groups of Quebec citizens wishing to remain part of Canada.

Quebec's Finance minister, Bernard Landry, has cited a 1992 legal opinion by five experts on international law commissioned by the Bélanger–Campeau Commission. This opinion concluded that the principle of territorial integrity meant that minorities would have no right to secede from an independent Quebec. Landry's citation is selective. The opinion also employed the same principle of territorial integrity to deny that Quebec had the right to secede from Canada. Moreover, it said that the right to self-determination was held only by colonized peoples, hardly the situation in Quebec, where the French-speaking majority controls the Quebec government and legislature.

BOUNDARY DEBATE

A subtheme of the partition debate addresses the issue of Quebec's borders. As the map below shows, the province of Quebec that joined Confederation in 1867 was much smaller – about one-third the size – than the current province.

Quebec's northern boundary has been extended twice since Confederation – in 1898 and 1912, on both occasions embracing land formerly part of the vast Rupert's Land territory, acquired by the Dominion government from the Hudson's Bay Company in 1870 (subsequently called the North-West Territories). At the time of the acquisition, the Canadian government made express commitments to "make adequate provision for the protection of the Indian tribes whose interests and well-being are involved in the transfer." This fiduciary duty clearly survived the two transfers of land to Quebec in 1898 and 1912.

Moreover, in 1912 the northern boundaries of Ontario and Manitoba as well as that of Quebec were extended.

Ostensibly, this was done to give the three provinces north-ern frontiers roughly comparable to the 60-degree-latitude boundaries awarded to the new provinces of Alberta and Saskatchewan. But the motivation also appears to have been an attempt to enable the provinces to better develop *as provinces* – the federal government of the day saw some value in having at least three provinces with equal access to Hudson Bay – and therefore to further unify and strengthen the federation. A *Globe and Mail* editorial on August 7, 1992, stated: "... the district of Ungava, covering the northern two-thirds of Quebec – including James Bay – was ceded to Quebec by acts of Parliament, *as part of Canada*. It was not meant as a going away present." Subsequently, the James Bay Cree, among others, have forcefully argued that both Canada and Quebec should have determined their wishes before proceeding with any boundary extension.

THE SUPREME COURT REFERENCE

During the 1995 referendum campaign, a former PQ sup-porter, Guy Bertrand, actively promoted the federalist cause, arguing that Quebec was indeed better off in Canada. Bertrand then brought a constitutional challenge against the PQ act respecting the future of Quebec (Bill 1), arguing that separation would be unconstitutional.

In a decision rendered on September 8, 1995, only weeks before the October 30, 1995, referendum vote, the Quebec Superior Court declared Bill 1 to be unconstitutional. The judge declared that the bill constituted a serious threat to the rights and freedoms of Bertrand guaranteed by the Canadian Charter, because the bill conferred on the Quebec National Assembly the power to proclaim Quebec a sover-eign country without following the amending procedures

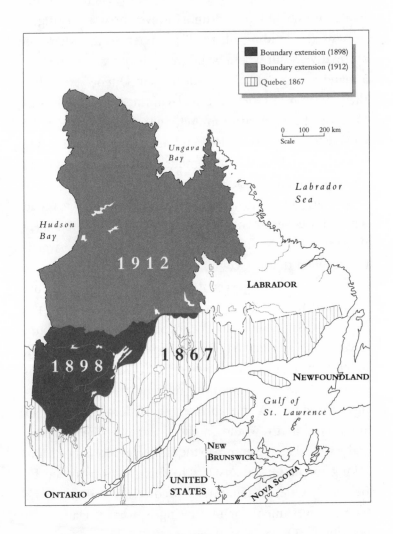

Quebec Boundaries, 1867-present

in the 1982 Constitution Act. The judge also noted that
Bertrand was not seeking to block Quebeckers from voting
in a consultative referendum. However, he was seeking to
prevent the holding of an illegal referendum where an
affirmative result would be taken by the PQ government as
a mandate to establish an independent Quebec state. For
the secession of Quebec to be legal the amending procedure of the Constitution Act, 1982 would have to be
altered to permit secession, and amending the amending
formula would require unanimous consent of all provinces
and Parliament.

The PQ government initially assigned a legal team to
defend the government's action. But when it appeared likely
that the court would side with Bertrand, the government
then argued that the courts had no jurisdiction to decide
such matters. In August 1996, the Quebec Superior Court
dismissed the Quebec government's attempt to have the
Bertrand case thrown out of court. Shortly after, the Quebec
government announced its withdrawal from the case and,
in effect, its rejection of the existing Constitution and thus
the rule of law in the event of a referendum result supporting sovereignty. A month later, the federal government
announced that it would, in effect, take over the challenge
and make a direct reference to the Supreme Court of Canada,
asking for definitive answers to the questions posed by
Bertrand. Quebec separatists predictably criticized the
federal government for interfering in what it claims is a
decision for Quebeckers alone.

In February 1998, the reference was argued before the
Supreme Court of Canada. The Court was asked to answer
three questions:

1. Under the Constitution of Canada, can the National Assembly, legislature, or government of Quebec effect the secession of Quebec from Canada unilaterally?

2. Does international law give the National Assembly, legislature, or government of Quebec the right to effect the secession of Quebec from Canada unilaterally? In this regard, is there a right of self-determination under international law that would give the National Assembly, legislature, or government of Quebec the right to effect the secession of Quebec from Canada unilaterally?

3. In the event of a conflict between domestic and international law on the right of the National Assembly, legislature, or government of Quebec to effect the secession of Quebec from Canada unilaterally, which would take precedence in Canada?

The federal government maintained that Quebeckers do have the right to determine their future so long as any independence referendum question is clear and fair, and the majority vote is sufficient. However, the federal government refused to specify *who* decides what is a fair question and what vote would be sufficient. The federal government also asserted, in pursuing the Supreme Court reference, that the Canadian Constitution must prevail – which means that Quebec could not secede unilaterally, but would have to negotiate its way out of the federation. The national government's hope was that, by emphasizing the serious legal and practical consequences of a Yes vote, it could persuade more Quebeckers to act cautiously in a future referendum.

The Quebec government refused to take part in the reference proceedings. The Supreme Court, therefore, appointed counsel – André Joli-Coeur – to represent Quebec. Joli-Coeur argued, among other things, that the court should not hear the reference, that the questions are hypothetical and primarily political in nature. While lawyers spoke and judges listened, demonstrators outside chanted and a small plane flew over the Supreme Court building, pulling a banner which read: "Le Québec aux Québécois."

In August 1998, in a unanimous decision, the Supreme Court essentially agreed with the federal government's arguments. It may be safely predicted that Quebec's PQ government will try to turn the result to political advantage. It is doubtful, however, that the decision, in the long run, will have much impact. Of much greater significance – as Quebeckers, and all Canadians, approach a third referendum – will be the political arguments and oratory on the value of being Canadian, arguments that will be made at the dawn of a new millennium when an entire new generation of Quebeckers is focussed on the world, on the global community and its networks, rather than on parochial provinces and tiresome federal–provincial battle-games whose warriors cannot unstick their feet from the cement of the past.

THREE-D: DECENTRALIZATION,
DEVOLUTION, DISTINCT SOCIETY
Shortly before the referendum, Prime Minister Chrétien made a speech at Verdun, setting out what has become known as the "Verdun promises." Chrétien said he was open to constitutional change. He then promised to fight for Quebec's recognition as a distinct society, and further changes, including federal withdrawal from labour-market

training. The Meech/Charlottetown refrain was starting up again.

Eventually, in November 1995, a motion was introduced in the House of Commons recognizing Quebec as a distinct society. It was accompanied by a bill to provide Quebec and four other regions with an effective veto over constitutional amendments (similar to the four regions proposed in the Victoria formula, except this time B.C. was a separate region).

Then, with the Speech from the Throne early in 1996, the federal government set out what is now known variously as "Plan A," "the devolutionist approach," or "the rebalancing of federal and provincial responsibilities." Ottawa promised not to initiate shared-cost programs in areas of exclusive provincial jurisdiction without majority approval from the premiers. Non-participating provinces would receive compensation "provided they establish equivalent or comparable initiatives." Ottawa also renounced its role in job training, transferring $2 billion to the provinces, at least one-quarter of which goes to Quebec. Finally, Ottawa announced that federal involvement in the area of forestry, mining, recreation, tourism, and social housing would be ended – the same areas listed in the abortive Charlottetown agreement.

That this strategy should so closely resemble the failed Charlottetown Accord should perhaps not be surprising, given that many of the top bureaucrats in the Chrétien government, up to and including the influential Clerk of the Privy Council, were all ascendant in the Charlottetown era under Mulroney.

Would the Canadian public be any more receptive to these proposals now than they were in 1992, if they were publicly debated? It seems unlikely. Nevertheless, the "devolutionist approach" fits the agenda of those who want to downsize government. These are the people who believe that the federal government is essentially helpless, that there is nothing it can do, especially in the social and cultural areas, while it is short of funds. Canadians are not assessing the devolution steps within the historical context, and perhaps out of exhaustion and the desire to engage in other more productive and relevant public debates, the current government appears poised to accomplish the Mulroney vision of Canada through stealth.

Certainly, there is little clear evidence that the federal government intends to reassert its presence in areas that may be critical to the long-term survival of Canada. These areas include a child-care initiative, environmental protection, and strengthening the economic union. An exception: in 1996, the federal government proposed to establish a long-overdue national securities commission. This proposal was promptly and noisily vetoed by British Columbia and Quebec, accompanied by facile arguments that a national body would not be sufficiently responsive to regional concerns.

The federal Liberals were re-elected with a reduced majority in June 1997, an election which resulted in the Reform Party replacing the Bloc Québécois as the official opposition and the traditional parties – the New Democrats and Progressive Conservatives – emerging with sufficiently increased representation to reacquire official-party status in the House of Commons.

On September 14, 1997, the premiers of nine provinces (Quebec's Lucien Bouchard was absent) and the leaders of the two territories agreed at a meeting in Calgary to a new framework for discussion on "Canadian unity." The seven points of the Calgary Declaration are:

- All Canadians are equal and have rights protected by law.
- All provinces, while diverse in their characteristics, have equality of status.
- Canada is graced by a diversity, tolerance, compassion and an equality of opportunity that is without rival in the world.
- Canada's gift of diversity includes Aboriginal peoples and cultures, the vitality of the English and French languages and a multicultural citizenry drawn from all parts of the world.
- In Canada's federal system, where respect for diversity and equality underlies unity, the unique character of Quebec society, including its French-speaking majority, its culture and its tradition of civil law, is fundamental to the well-being of Canada. Consequently, the legislature and government of Quebec have a role to protect and develop the unique character of Quebec society within Canada.
- If any further constitutional amendment confers powers on one province, these powers must be available to all provinces.
- Canada is a federal system where federal, provincial and territorial governments work in partnership while respecting each other's jurisdictions. Canadians want their governments to work cooperatively and with flexibility to ensure the efficiency and effectiveness of the federation. Canadians want their governments to work together particularly in the delivery of their social programs. Provinces and territories renew their commitment to work in partnership with the government of Canada to best serve the needs of Canadians.

Within days of the declaration being made public, aboriginal peoples voiced anger and dismay at having their
interests dealt with merely as part of Canada's "gift of diversity."* The premiers quickly recognized their error (remarkably similar to the error they made in dismissing aboriginal
peoples in the initial Meech Lake Accord – one wonders
how they can do it twice) and negotiated a quick retreat.
Although it was too late, the premiers said, to reopen the
wording of the declaration, they agreed to append a companion aboriginal document to the declaration which would
be submitted as a package to the public-consultation process.
They also agreed to "consider" the aboriginal document
when it came time to submit the declaration to their legislatures for endorsement. The document states that aboriginal people possess the inherent right of self-government. It
states that Canada is a "federal system in which federal,
provincial, territorial and aboriginal governments work in
partnership while respecting each other's jurisdictions, rights
and responsibilities." It says that aboriginal men and women
are equal, and it enshrines aboriginals' right to protect and
develop "their languages, cultures and identities," identical
language to what appeared in the Charlottetown Accord.

Provincial consultation with the public fell short of
attracting enthusiastic interest. Nevertheless, as of June
1998, all provincial legislatures had endorsed the declaration,

---

* Canada's aboriginal peoples were, you will recall, to be considered "one
of three orders of government in Canada," according to the Charlottetown
Accord, and the "inherent" governments – the gift of no one – of aboriginal people would have the authority to "safeguard and develop
their languages, cultures, economics identities and traditions" and to
"develop, maintain and strengthen their relationship with their lands,
water and environment."

except Quebec, which has condemned it as a non-starter. It has the support of the federal government because, in the minds of Ottawa's constitutional generals, its tone and direction are a good fit with Plan A, which – since the Supreme Court reference in February and the noisy attention it attracted from Quebec nationalists – is emerging as the government's favoured strategy. In a speech to the Liberal party policy convention in March 1998, the Prime Minister placed a great deal of emphasis on Plan A: the transfer of powers to the provinces on job-training, a new federal–provincial agreement on the environment, and the constitutional amendments allowing Quebec and Newfoundland to abolish denominational school boards. According to the Prime Minister: "This is an impressive list – and a long one – and it proves Canada is capable of the sort of radical changes separatists always assert are necessary."

In the spring of 1998, the national Progressive Conservative party leader, Jean Charest, jumped to the leadership of the Quebec Liberal party. In a gesture meant to be supportive, Ottawa's Minister of Human Resources, Pierre Pettigrew (who refers to himself as a "Plan A minister"), emphasized that the best way to help Charest win the hearts and minds of Quebeckers for the federalist cause is to engineer federal and provincial co-operation on policies that matter to Canadians' everyday lives: code-language for devolution.

The Plan A devolution strategy is guided more by political expedience and federal–provincial power struggles than by the long-term interests of the nation, Canada. Consider the environment, for example. In early 1998, a harmonization accord on federal–provincial environmental jurisdiction was signed in St. John's by the federal government and all provinces except Quebec (the ostensible target of the devolution, which rejected the accord because it did not go far enough). Ottawa agreed to the harmonization accord even though, weeks earlier, in December 1997, Parliament's all-party standing committee on the environment had urged the government *not* to proceed with it because there was no proof of overlap and duplication in regulatory policies by the two levels of government. Rather, the committee found that so-called harmonization would virtually remove the federal government from environmental protection and thus weaken it across the country. The federal minister and her cabinet colleagues chose to ignore the committee's recommendations.

The accord touches every aspect of environmental protection, from inspection activities and regulatory controls to the development of Canada-wide standards on air, water, and soil quality; from emissions of benzine, mercury, and dioxins to standards on ground-level ozone. Subagreements between the two levels of governments will permit the provinces to assume responsibility for inspections, standards, environmental assessments, monitoring, and enforcement. Not all provinces will assume new powers and responsibilities at the same pace, but the direction is inexorably one-way.

It was signed at a time when serious concerns have been raised about the provinces' ability to enforce existing regulations. While Environment Canada – the federal department – has lost 30 per cent of its budget due to cutbacks over the past two years, most provincial agencies have suffered worse cuts: Newfoundland's ministry has lost 65 per cent of its budget, Quebec's 65 per cent, Ontario's 44 per cent, and Alberta's 37 per cent. Several days before the St. John's meeting, three major environmental protection organizations – including the Quebec Environmental Law Centre

– made public the results of a study showing the dangers of the federal government transferring responsibility for environmental monitoring and protection to the provinces. Since 1994, the report said, a federal–Quebec agreement has given the Quebec government primary responsibility for administering and enforcing federal environmental regulations. Yet Quebec has failed to take *any* action against consistent violations of federal pulp-and-paper-mill effluent regulations (189 violations by 20 mills in 1996 alone).

Given this snapshot of a provincial enforcement record, the words of Charles Caccia, former Liberal federal Environment minister and chairman of the Commons environment committee, are chilling in their understatement: "It is difficult to resist the observation that we are witnessing a disturbing trend [when] the environment is perceived as . . . incompatible with national unity."

In a similar approach on social policy, the federal government put forward a "national child benefit" scheme at the 1996 First Ministers' Conference with the aim of having a framework in place for discussion at the 1998 conference. While some progress towards this and what is broadly known as the "social union" has been made, most informed observers have noted that Ottawa lost substantial leverage over the design of the benefit and social policy generally when it effectively abandoned involvement in provincial welfare policy by replacing the Canada Assistance Plan with the Canada Health and Social Transfer. Under CAP, federal money was tied, more or less, to national welfare standards. Under the CHST, national standards were promised and later abandoned. The unanswered question – in this area and others – is whether these initiatives will allow the federal government to rebuild meaningful and necessary social policies, or whether the Meech–Charlottetown bureaucrats who hold sway in the upper reaches of the Privy Council Office (notably, Jocelyne Bourgon, Clerk of the Privy Council) and elsewhere in Ottawa will succeed in further marginalizing the federal government in the "interests" of "national unity."

POLLS, POLLS, POLLS

Quebeckers' ambivalence about the country and their place in it continues to frustrate policy makers on both sides. As Quebec comedian Michel Courtmanche has said, Quebeckers' ideal is an independent Quebec within a strong, united Canada. In April 1998, a poll by CROP in Quebec and by Environics Research Group in the rest of Canada – conducted for the Council for Canadian Unity – found that 75 per cent of Quebec respondents described themselves as very attached or somewhat attached to Canada. The attachment, admittedly, was greater in the Maritimes (97 per cent), Ontario (96 per cent), and the West (95 per cent). Nevertheless, the poll confirms a reluctance on the part of Quebeckers to choose between Quebec and Canada. Indeed, only 20 per cent of francophone respondents in the province agreed with the statement "I am not attached to Canada and I would prefer that Quebec stopped being part of Canada." In the same poll, 77 per cent of Quebeckers said they would vote Yes on the question "Do you want Quebec to remain a province in Canada?"

As in the past, however, the poll confirms Quebeckers' confusion about Quebec sovereignty in the context of an economic partnership with the rest of Canada (as proposed in the 1995 referendum). Thirty-seven per cent of

Quebec respondents indicated they did not think such a partnership would mean Quebec would leave Canada and become independent; 29 per cent thought Quebec would still elect members of Parliament to Ottawa; 39 per cent said Quebeckers would still be Canadian citizens; and 36 per cent said Quebec would still be a province of Canada.

Another recent poll, by Leger and Leger, showed that 64 per cent of Quebec respondents wanted to be consulted in a referendum on the Calgary Declaration, and that, if Jean Charest were elected premier, he should enter into negotiations to renew the Constitution. More than half (52 per cent) then said Charest should put the results of these negotiations to a referendum vote. There is nothing surprising to all this – as confusing, and even contradictory, as it might appear. Given the similarities between the Calgary Declaration and the Meech and Charlottetown accords, one would be more surprised if Canadians in every province did not want a referendum on the proposals from Calgary.

AND SO, FROM HERE

While many Canadians – the authors of this book among them – decry the retreat of their national government from national life, the economist Thomas Courchene notes that Ottawa's powers are being devolved both downwards to the provinces and upwards to global and regional trade bodies (labour and environmental policies under NAFTA, for example), to such a degree and at such a pace that "a decade from now, no one will care if Quebec separates." The ties that bind – or once bound – are everywhere loosening, and the country has journeyed far from Sir John A. Macdonald's National Policy of high tariffs and a transcontinental railway aimed at strengthening the Canadian economic union against American influence and pull. Recently, daily train service was resurrected between Vancouver and Seattle, five years after Via Rail cancelled daily service from Vancouver to eastern Canada. Provincial export trade, especially to the United States, has increased exponentially and now swamps interprovincial trade. Quebec exports 34 per cent more outside the country than it does to the rest of Canada; Ontario's international exports are more than twice the value of its interprovincial trade. The Reform Party, the official opposition in Parliament, would end official bilingualism, making language and culture provincial matters, and ultimately leave the federal government with only defence, foreign affairs, mobility rights, trading standards, commercial and competition law, and the post office. The second main opposition party, the Bloc Québécois, is committed to Canada's destruction. The once-powerful Tories are irrelevant, and even the NDP has all but vanished from the national dialogue. It is perhaps not surprising that the federal government's approach to the provinces is marked by a confused, tentative caution.

And yet it is by no means an unchallengeable proposition that the national government should continue its withdrawal from national life. More powers to provincial governments will simply make Canadians less capable of influencing the very forces (global and otherwise) that are provoking today's frustrating sense of powerlessness. The provincial track record with respect to co-ordinating national policies and national standards is not encouraging. And what does seem apparent is that national leaders are incapable of thinking clearly about the role of the federal government and the uses of federal power. This need not be,

their long-term survival as a largely francophone society in North America is enhanced by Canada's protection of minority-language rights and its commitment to official bilingualism.

Distinct society for Quebec? Special status for Quebec? It is no route to constitutional peace and it should be set aside. It is without, as this book has shown, persuasive legal, historical, or constitutional foundation, notwithstanding the ceaseless dialectics and contentions of the enthusiasts for Meech, Charlottetown, and Calgary. The vision of Pierre Trudeau is not an aberration; it is consistent with history – a federal Canada in which the division of powers applies uniformly to all provinces, with multiculturalism, institutional bilingualism, and individual rights guaranteed in a Charter of Rights and Freedoms.

Two commandments: end the unrelenting devolution of powers; bury distinct society.

The unrelenting devolution of powers, however incremental and supposedly non-constitutional it may be labelled – a little side-deal here, a smallish bilateral agreement there – is leading inexorably to an ineffective, irrelevant national government prodded meekly to the margins of Canadians' lives. Not only Quebeckers but, increasingly, Canadians elsewhere look more to their provincial governments for the agendas of state. If this continues, provincial communities will in time dominate and replace the national community and, inevitably, Quebec separation will seem like a small, logical, unsurprising step. When we look back across our history, moreover, we can see that concessions to the provinces, especially Quebec, have been substantial. To name a few: Laurier's refusal to intervene (as explicitly permitted by the Constitution Act, 1867) in the Manitoba separate schools issue; the Privy Council's judicial tilt in the provinces' favour; Mackenzie King's failure to establish a strong, national, social policy net as recommended by the Marsh Report; the St. Laurent government's approval of provincial paramountcy in the concurrent federal–provincial jurisdiction over pensions; the Pearson government's approval of Quebec opting out of national shared-cost programs.

Only during the years of the Trudeau administration was there a concerted and persistent attempt to reverse decentralization (we allow a possible exception for John Diefenbaker's "One Canada" campaigns), and the vigorous assertion of federal powers combined with the promotion of Canada's bilingual face, multiculturalism, and constitutional protections of individual rights brought positive results. Following the 1980 referendum and the 1982 constitutional reforms, support for Quebec separatism dropped significantly.

The Mulroney government reinstated – with a vengeance – the devolutionist trend. The Mulroney government divided Canadians with Meech and Charlottetown. It then weakened the country with bilateral federal–provincial agreements, with its preoccupation with cultural and economic integration with the United States, and with its absence of any unifying vision of Canada.

The Chrétien government came to office in 1993 having pledged to undo the damage wrought in the Mulroney years. The pledge proved hollow. The government found itself immersed in economic issues and overwhelmed by pro-Meech, pro-Charlottetown bureaucrats who have continued to guide it along Meech-by-the-back-door pathways.

No nation carries divine assurance of immortality. Perhaps Canada – lacking visionary federal leadership and a strong federalist presence in Quebec – cannot avoid decline and eventual disintegration. Not much can be done to build a country without a dream to match, without will and vision, without determination and courage. We believe, however, that a new generation of Canadians, Quebeckers among them, is transcendent. It is a generation focussed on the world, not on provinces. It sees a promise in Canadian society that eclipses the parochial and the tired debates of petty satraps. It is a generation that sees value in the Canadian society that has been created by Canadian visionaries – the Canadian society of the Charter of Rights, official bilingualism, multiculturalism, the peaceful, orderly national society of national standards, national health, national well-being. If this generation has its way, Canada will thrive.

INDEX

Page numbers in italic indicate a figure or map. The italic letter *n* following a page number indicates that the information can be found in a footnote on that page.

Canada, Quebec, and the Uses of Nationalism, Second Edition
Ramsay Cook

"Cook is cogent and incisive. . . ."   – *Calgary Herald*

The quiet nationalism of English Canada, standing stubbornly against the might of the United States; the proud nationalism of Quebec, obsessed with its survival in an Anglo-dominated continent; and the fierce nationalism of Canada's First Nations, born out of its long, troubled history with European settlers – in a timely and important book about the clash of cultures in Canada, noted historian Ramsay Cook examines nationalism as the pivotal factor in our country's history and development. Featuring eight new chapters and an updated introduction, *Canada, Quebec, and the Uses of Nationalism* is essential reading for anyone interested in Canada's past, present, and future.

Trade paperback • 6 x 9 • 312 pages • $19.99

The Essential Trudeau
Pierre Trudeau. Edited by Ron Graham

More than any other prime minister in Canadian history, Pierre Trudeau had an approach to practical politics that began from a strong philosophical base. Now, for the first time, Trudeau's thoughts on a variety of themes, from democracy and nationalism to free enterprise and federalism, are brought together in a systematic, easy-to-read, pocket-sized format. To this finely honed selection has been added a new commentary, including introductory notes to each thematic section and reflections on such contemporary developments as the rise of neo-conservatism and the most recent nationalistic excesses of the Parti Québécois.

Cloth • 4½ x 8 • 240 pages • $19.99

Trudeau and Our Times:
Volume 1: The Magnificent Obsession
Stephen Clarkson and Christina McCall

"In prose that is lucid and gripping, the authors . . . have brought the public and private selves of Pierre Trudeau together, illuminating in the process his overwhelming impact on the country's political life."
— Citation, Governor General's Literary Award

The Magnificent Obsession examines the formative influences on Pierre Trudeau's childhood, his knight-errant youth and early manhood, his charismatic ascent to the Liberal Party leadership, and his dramatic first decade as prime minister. It concludes with a compelling account of his bittersweet triumphs in fighting off the separatists in the 1980 Quebec referendum campaign and his battle with provincial premiers to patriate the Canadian constitution.

Trade paperback • 6 x 9 • 504 pages • $21.99

Trudeau and Our Times:
Volume 2: The Heroic Delusion
Stephen Clarkson and Christina McCall

"Mandatory reading for all Canadians trying to understand that most difficult of all times to grasp, the recent past."
— *Vancouver Sun*

This volume describes in fascinating detail the abiding liberal Pierre Trudeau's quixotic confrontations with his neo-conservative opponents, Margaret Thatcher and Ronald Reagan. A masterful analysis of the country's political economy in the decades following the Second World War, it suggests that Trudeau's delusion was that Canada could pursue a policy independent of her neighbour to the south.

Trade paperback • 6 x 9 • 592 pages • $21.99
Also Available: Boxed Set, Volumes 1 and 2 • $39.99

Nationalism Without Walls:
The Unbearable Lightness of Being Canadian
Richard Gwyn

"Speaks eloquently about who we are."   – Montreal *Gazette*

In this profound examination of Canadian nationhood, Richard Gwyn asks whether we have it in us to reinvent our identity so that we remain a true community of communities that is larger than the sum of its parts. Believing that no nation is more vulnerable to global change than Canada, Gwyn puts forward some surprising propositions: that NAFTA has become a *de facto* sovereignty-association pact, that the Charter of Rights and Freedoms promotes inequality, and, in a powerful chapter, that much of what is laudable about Canada has arisen from the traditions and values of English Canada. *Nationalism Without Walls* is always original, provocative, and unexpected.

Trade paperback • 6 x 9 • 304 pages • $19.99

Against the Current: Selected Writings 1939-1996
Pierre Trudeau. Edited by Gérard Pelletier

"*Against the Current* challenges us . . . to think through the demands of our common life with clearheadedness, and daring, and will. . . . It deserves close study."   – *Toronto Star*

Pierre Trudeau has described himself as a man who has always paddled against the current, always aiming to test the strength of prevailing ideas. From his earliest articles and essays to the thunderous salvoes fired at the advocates of the Meech Lake and the Charlottetown accords, Trudeau's writing has been marked by an unremitting commitment to democracy, equality, and justice. In *Against the Current*, he and Gérard Pelletier brought together a superb collection of Trudeau's writing that constitutes an intellectual portrait of a man whose ideas have shaped not only his own life, but the country he has represented and served.

Cloth • 6½ x 9¼ • 352 pages • $35.00

The Canadian Way: Shaping Canada's Foreign Policy, 1968-1984
Ivan Head and Pierre Trudeau

"... valuable for both its vision and its perspective. It represents a view of Canada and the world between 1968 and 1984 from two persons who largely shaped it."   – *Globe and Mail*

In the years between 1968 and 1984, Prime Minister Pierre Trudeau decided to use Canada's unique position and reputation to increase its potential as an "effective" diplomatic power. Trudeau worked closely with Ivan Head, a former law professor, who was his right-hand man in shaping the country's foreign policy. This book, written jointly by Head and Trudeau, is a frank account of the successes and failures they experienced and the problems they encountered as the world changed around them. *The Canadian Way* provides a fascinating insider's view of an important period in the development of Canada's foreign policy.

Cloth • 6½ x 9¼ • 380 pages • $29.99

1759: The Battle for Canada
Laurier L. LaPierre

"More Canadians than ever will know what really happened in 1759, and come away with a few insights into why we're still fighting that war."   – *Toronto Star*

The battle of the Plains of Abraham was a watershed in the history of Canada. In *1759*, Laurier LaPierre, historian and passionate Canadian, acts as a commentator and guide as he recreates for readers the momentous events of a few weeks in the summer of 1759, when two European powers fought for control of the fledging nation of Canada on the banks of the St. Lawrence. LaPierre fleshes out the bare bones of historical fact with imaginative stories and interviews and breathes life into this dramatic moment in our past. Never before has Canadian history been quite so vivid – or so provocative.

Trade paperback • 6 x 9 • 304 pages • $16.99

No Holds Barred: My Life in Politics
John C. Crosbie

"May set the standard for frank, compelling and important autobiography. . . . A must read." — *Financial Post*

John Crosbie served at the highest levels in this country as minister of finance, transport, justice, international trade, and fisheries and oceans, and he became famous as a politician unlike others, someone with a sharp tongue, who has always spoken his mind.

In *No Holds Barred*, Crosbie offers trenchant opinions on issues ranging from Atlantic Canada's prospects to Canada's relationship with Cuba. He also offers his penetrating and unflinching assessments of politicians he has known. Nothing is withheld in this entertaining memoir by one of the dominant political figures of his generation.

Trade paperback • 6 x 9 • 512 pages • $19.99

Memoirs
Pierre Trudeau

"Pure Trudeau – witty, arrogant, intelligent, and partisan . . . a must read for anyone interested in this country."

— *Calgary Sun*

Conversational and informal in tone, in this autobiography Pierre Trudeau takes us through his life, concentrating on his sixteen years as Canada's prime minister. Enriching this very personal book are 253 photographs, 106 of them in full colour. Many of them – from official sources or private family albums – have never before been published. As prime minister between 1968 and 1984, Pierre Trudeau changed your life; now is your chance to read about his life in this book that belongs in every Canadian home.

Trade paperback • 6½ x 9¼ • 382 pages • $19.99